Heinemann History Scheme

LIFE IN MEDIEVAL TIMES

BOOK 1

Judith Kidd

Rosemary Rees

Ruth Tudor

D1355039

Heinemann

Heinemann Educational Publishers
Halley Court, Jordan Hill, Oxford, OX2 8EJ
a division of Reed Educational & Professional Publishing Ltd
Heinemann is a registered trademark of Reed Educational & Professional Publishing Ltd

OXFORD MELBOURNE AUCKLAND
JOHANNESBURG BLANTYRE GABORONE
IBADAN PORTSMOUTH NH (USA) CHICAGO

© Heinemann Educational Publishers 2000

First published 2000

ISBN 0 435 32594 9

02 01 00
10 9 8 7 6 5 4 3 2 1

Designed and typeset by Visual Image, Taunton

Illustrated by Paul Bale, Jane Durston and Ian Heard

Printed and bound in Spain by Edelvives

Picture research by Diana Phillips

Photographic acknowledgements

The authors and publishers would like to thank the following for permission to reproduce photographs and copyright material:

Aerofilms: p. 65 (both); Art Archive: pp. 21, 36, 53, 58, 100 (left), 108 (top); Bridgeman Art Library: pp. 16, 66, 80, 106, 139, 142, 148, 149, 189, 190; British Library: pp. 105 (both), 107 (both); Bodleian Library: pp. 108 (bottom), 117; Buckinghamshire Record Office: p. 67; Collections: p. 91 (bottom); Corpus Christi College, Cambridge: p. 183; Fotomas: p. 154
Sonia Halliday: pp. 72, 87, 90 (all), 91 (top), 94 (both), 98, 168, 169, 172, 173, 177 (top), 191; M Holford: pp. 29, 30; A F Kersting: pp. 34, 44, 100 (bottom); Kobal: p. 84; Photodisc: p. 15; Punch: p. 17; Rex Features/Sipa: p. 184; Saltaire Village Society: p. 24 (left)
Science Photo Library: p. 18; Skyscan: pp. 22, 74; Spectrum: pp. 24 (right), 174 (both).

Cover photograph: © The Bodleian Library

Maps and realia
Map reproduced from Ordnance Survey maps with the permission of The Controller of Her Majesty's Stationery Office
© Crown Copyright: p. 35; English Heritage: p. 103 (bottom); Whee Ky Ma: p. 14 (top).

Written source acknowledgements
The authors and publishers gratefully acknowledge the following publications from which written sources in the book are drawn. In some sources the wording or sentence has been simplified.

H S Bennett, *Life on the English Manor*, Cambridge University Press, 1937: p. 95 (bottom left)
M T Clanchy, *England and its rulers*, Fontana 1983: p. 33
R J Cootes, *The Middle Ages*, Longman, 1972: p. 66 (top right)
A H Dodd, *Life in Elizabethan England*, Batsford, 1961: p. 133
G Evans, *Pilgrimages and Crusades*, 1976: p. 184 (left)
H E Hallam, *Rural England*, Fontana, 1981: p. 66 (top left)
A Harmsworth, *Elizabethan England*, John Murray, 1999: p. 141
T Jones & A Ereria, *The Crusades*, BBC Books, 1994: pp. 164, 184 (right)
M H Keen, *England in the Later Middle Ages*, Routledge, 1973: p. 95 (bottom right)
J Kerr, *The Crusades*, Wheaton, 1966: p. 179
B Lewis, *Islam, from the Prophet Muhammad to the capture of Constantinople*, Harper & Row, 1974: p. 162
H R Loyn, *Anglo-Saxon England and the Norman Conquest*, Longman, 1962: p. 66 (bottom right)

J Nicol, *The Tudors*, Blackwell, 1981: p. 155 (bottom)
G Regan, *Elizabethan England*, Batsford, 1990: p. 138 (top)
P Servini, *The English Reformation*, Hodder & Stoughton, 1997: p. 131 (both)
C Shepherd (ed.), *Contrasts and connections*, John Murray, 1991: pp. 50, 51
C Shepherd et al, *Societies in change*, John Murray, 1992: p. 137 (bottom)
S Styles, *Elizabethan England*, Heinemann, 1992: pp. 137 (top), 138 (bottom), 155 (top)
The Times, 5 June 1913: p. 15 (right)
The Times, 1987: p. 105 (bottom)
The Mirror, 14 February 2000: p. 19
D Wilkinson & J Cantrell, *Normans in Britain*, Macmillan Press Ltd, 1987: pp. 41, 62, 64.

Contents

Unit 1: Introductory unit – what's it all about?

EDEN

RUSSIA

ESTONIA
LATVIA
BELARUS
UKRAINE

HUNGARY
ROMANIA
BULGARIA
TURKEY
ECE
SYRIA
IRAQ

KAZAKSTAN

TURKMENISTAN
UZBEKISTAN
KYRGYZSTAN

MONGOLIA

NORTH
KOREA

JAPAN

SOUTH
KOREA

IRAN

AFGHANISTAN

PAKISTAN

CHINA

NEPAL
BHUTAN

PACIFIC
OCEAN

EGYPT
SAUDI
ARABIA

OMAN

INDIA

LAOS

MYANMAR

AD
SUDAN

CENTRAL
AFRICAN
PUBLIC

ERITREA
SOUTHERN YEMEN
YEMEN
SOMALIA
ETHIOPIA

UGANDA
KENYA

EM. REP.
OF THE
CONGO
TANZANIA

RWANDA
BURUNDI
MALAWI

BANGLADESH

THAILAND

VIETNAM

CAMBODIA

PHILIPPINES

MALAYSIA

INDONESIA

PAPUA
NEW
GUINEA

A
ZAMBIA

MOZAMBIQUE

INDIAN
OCEAN

MADAGASCAR

AUSTRALIA

NEW
CALEDONIA

OUTH
RICA

SWAZILAND
LESOTHO

NEW
ZEALAND

SOUTHERN OCEAN

A JOURNEY THROUGH TIME

You will investigate some of these events in this book. Remember though, that it is difficult to be precise about the beginning of some of these events.

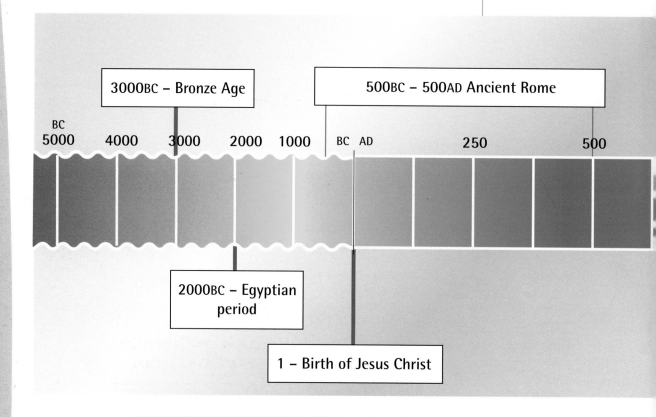

3000BC – Bronze Age

500BC – 500AD Ancient Rome

| BC 5000 | 4000 | 3000 | 2000 | 1000 | BC AD | 250 | 500 |

2000BC – Egyptian period

1 – Birth of Jesus Christ

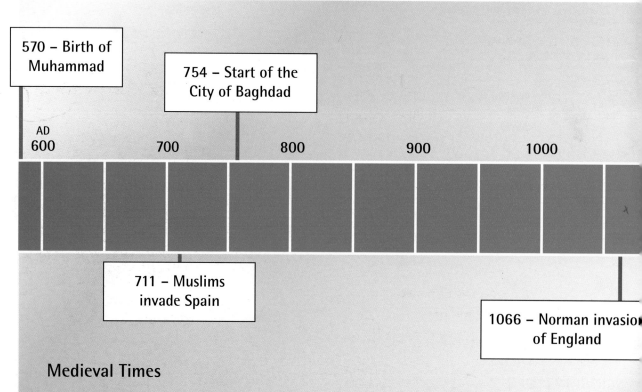

570 – Birth of Muhammad

754 – Start of the City of Baghdad

| AD 600 | 700 | 800 | 900 | 1000 |

711 – Muslims invade Spain

1066 – Norman invasion of England

Medieval Times

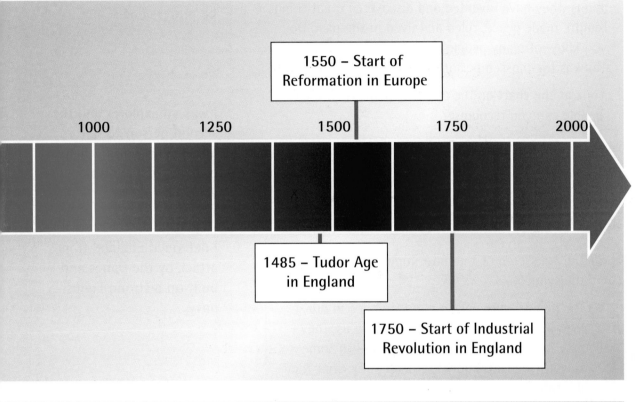

1550 – Start of
Reformation in Europe

1000   1250   1500   1750   2000

1485 – Tudor Age
in England

1750 – Start of Industrial
Revolution in England

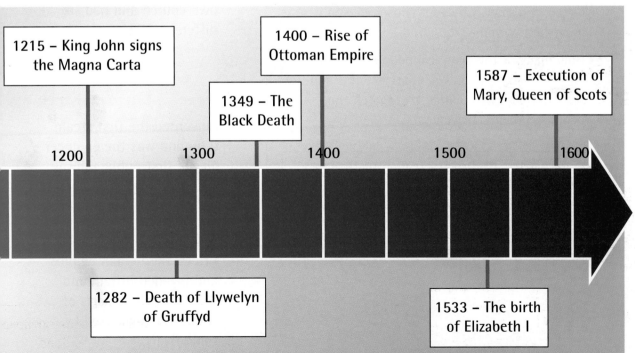

1215 – King John signs
the Magna Carta

1400 – Rise of
Ottoman Empire

1587 – Execution of
Mary, Queen of Scots

1349 – The
Black Death

1200   1300   1400   1500   1600

1282 – Death of Llywelyn
of Gruffyd

1533 – The birth
of Elizabeth I

WHO IS THE MOST IMPORTANT PERSON I KNOW ABOUT IN HISTORY?

History is all about people. People make things happen and change our lives. Famous people in the past have done funny, shocking, amazing and very important things. They have invented and discovered great things, fought, made peace, ruled and lived in the past. Do you know of many people in history? Who do you think is the most important person in the past?

Look at the chart on the opposite page. How many people can you recognise?

Activity Time

❶ Draw a sketch of the most important person that you know.

❷ The people who make a big difference in our lives are often the most important to us. They may have given us ideas or helped us in some way. Or, we can simply like people for what they do. Label your picture to show at least three different reasons why your chosen person is so important to you.

❸ How many of the historical people in Source 1 do you recognise? Draw a chart like this and use the information in Source 1 to match the people to their achievements:

Person	What are they famous for?

SOURCE 1

I looked after wounded soldiers in the Crimean War and trained nurses to be professionals.

I was an explorer and the second person to sail around the world. I helped to beat the Spanish Armada.

I defended England from attack by the Danes and built up a strong English navy.

I ruled England, set up my own church and had six different wives.

I invented the first steam train and was the engineer on the first public railway.

I ruled the Roman Empire and invaded Britain and Gaul, as well as parts of Asia. I was murdered by some rivals.

FLORENCE NIGHTINGALE

QUEEN VICTORIA

ALEXANDER THE GREAT

I was King of Greece and expanded my empire to Persia and Egypt.

I wrote many plays and poems that are still popular in the twenty-first century.

HENRY VIII

SIR FRANCIS DRAKE

WILLIAM SHAKESPEARE

I tried to blow up the Houses of Parliament but was caught, tortured and executed.

GEORGE STEPHENSON

GUY FAWKES

KING ALFRED

I ruled for 64 years when Britain had a great empire all over the world.

I led the south-east of England in a revolt against the Romans. I poisoned myself rather than be killed by them.

JULIUS CAESAR

BOUDICCA

ELIZABETH 1

I made England wealthy and successful when I was queen. I was very popular, but I never married.

TIME CHECK

We measure time in many different ways. To help us to make sense of the past, we split it up into different periods or eras, like the Stone Age, the Middle Ages and the Victorian period. Periods can be named after what materials or objects were made from at that time or which country or family was in charge. Sometimes to be more exact, we use centuries or decades to refer to times in the past. These tasks will check that you understand time and how we split it up into sections in history. The timeline on pages 6 and 7 can be used in any history lesson to put people and events into chronological order (order of time).

Activity Time

1 Some of the periods have been labelled on the timeline on pages 6 and 7. Others have been left out. Write out each of these periods on slips of paper and try to place them in chronological order on the timeline. Look up the periods in a textbook or reference book if you are stuck.

a Stone Age
b Iron Age
c eighteenth century

d The Stuarts
e The Ancient Greeks
f 1960s

2 Do you know of any historical periods or eras that are missing from the timeline? Make a list of any more time periods that you can think of.

3 Can you think of two reasons why this timeline does not include every period in history? Explain your ideas.

4 What do you think that people in the future will call the time from 1950–2000? Try to think of two different suggestions.

Activity Time

Famous people, famous times.

Can you place all the famous people we have met so far in the correct place in time? Do you think that some time periods contain more famous people than others? Let's find out.

1 Do you know when all the people in Source 1 on pages 8 and 9 were famous?
a Write each person's name on a slip of paper and try to put them into chronological order (order of time) on the timeline on pages 6 and 7. There are some key words on the timeline to help you.
b Beside each person on your chart write down the century or time period that they were from. You may need to get help from a textbook, library book, an encyclopaedia or your teacher.

c There are more people on your chart from the 1500s than from any other period. Does this mean that it is the time when most happened in history? Explain your answer.

2 Work in pairs to decide who is the most important person in history. It does not have to be anyone from pages 8 and 9 and you can disagree with your partner. Discuss all the different reasons why you have chosen your person to appear in History's Hall of Fame. Be prepared to explain your reasons to the rest of the class.

WHAT MAKES PEOPLE IMPORTANT IN HISTORY?

People make history: heroes, villains, leaders, inventors, explorers, and people with new ideas. You probably found it very hard to decide who was most important. Now think about a very hard question: what makes some people more important than others? Would you choose the person from the best story, the one you remember most or someone whom we still mention today?

Activity Time

1 Who does your class think are the top three most important people in history? Do a survey to find out.

2 In your survey find out what aspects your class thinks makes a person important in history. How many chose people who:

a are important for helping to make a country great?

b are important for helping lots of people?

c are important for changing history in a big way?

d are important for setting an example to other people?

e are important for doing something which you are interested in?

f are important for something unusual or which is part of a good story?

3 Draw a sketch of your chosen person to hang in the History Hall of Fame. Include a decorated picture frame to make them look important. It could even have symbols or pictures on it, with objects from their life and work. Write a paragraph underneath to explain why you have chosen this person. Include these points:
- what they are famous for
- three reasons why you think they are so important
- why they are more important than another person from the chart on pages 8 and 9.

Who deserves to appear in History's Hall of Fame?

THE POPULARITY TEST

Compare four people from history and try to decide who is the most important. Work in pairs, then see if you agree with the rest of the class.

SOURCE 2

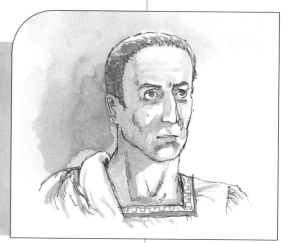

JULIUS CAESAR

Julius Caesar was one of the leaders of Rome as it was expanding to become an empire. As a general he was famous for winning battles. He invaded Gaul (France), Britain and Asia Minor. He ruled Rome on his own from 46 to 44 BC when he was stabbed to death by some enemies. His great-nephew became the very first Roman emperor.

SOURCE 3

QUEEN ELIZABETH I

Elizabeth ruled England from 1558 to 1603. She introduced laws to make the religion of the country Protestant and was also famous for bringing in laws to make parishes (towns and villages) look after the poor. England became a wealthier country under Elizabeth's rule. Trade with, and knowledge about, the rest of the world increased. The Armada, the fleet of ships sent from Spain by its government carrying soldiers to invade England, failed when Elizabeth was queen. She liked entertainment and encouraged plays and poems to be written. Elizabeth is famous for having her cousin, Mary Queen of Scots, executed, to stop Mary from being a threat to her rule. She was strict with any rebels, and had the Earl of Essex executed in 1601.

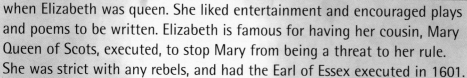

SOURCE 4

GUY FAWKES

Guy Fawkes was part of a plot to blow up Parliament in November 1605. He was a Catholic and was unhappy about King James's harsh treatment of Catholics. He was caught in a cellar underneath the Houses of Parliament with some explosives, ready to blow up the king, Parliament and all the MPs. He was discovered after an anonymous letter (a letter with no signature to say who it was from) was shown to the king's minister. He was tortured, confessed to his part in the plot and was executed. He helped to make Catholics more unpopular in England. In Britain the night he was caught, 5 November, is still remembered every year as Bonfire Night, with fires and fireworks.

SOURCE 5

GEORGE STEPHENSON

George Stephenson was an engineer. He invented the very first steam train and designed the style of railway tracks now used all over the world. He worked for one of the very first railway companies in England on the Manchester to Liverpool line. The company set up a competition to find the best engine which Stephenson won with his engine, called 'The Rocket'. He then worked as an engineer for other new railway companies, helping to make transport and travel much quicker.

Activity Time

❶ Copy and fill in this chart to find out which person you think is more important:

Person	This person made a big difference to the world by...	Without this person we would not...	We are still affected by this person today because...
Julius Caesar			
Elizabeth I			
Guy Fawkes			
George Stephenson			

❷ Guy Fawkes is not important; he was a criminal and a loser. Do you agree?

❸ Explain which person on the chart above you think is the most important and share your reasons with the rest of the class.

❹ How many people on the chart on pages 8 and 9 are women? Why do you think that there are many more famous men in history than women?

Summary

People make our history. But it is not just famous people that make a difference. When you come across new people in your History lessons remember to think about why they are important and the effects they have had.

WHAT ARE WE GOING TO FIND OUT ABOUT IN HISTORY IN YEARS 7, 8 AND 9?

History is based on many different types of evidence, called sources. Historians use written, visual and oral (spoken) sources, artefacts (objects) and ICT to find out about the past. Some examples of sources are letters, diaries, photographs, buildings and poems. See if you can think of at least six more sources of evidence that historians use. You will have used some of them in earlier history lessons. Historians use sources to piece together clues or evidence about the past.

The sources below give us a few clues about what we are going to investigate in history lessons. Your job is to act like a historian and use these sources to work out some of the stories that we will study. Because historians are like detectives, you will have to ask some questions to find out some answers . Be warned though – we don't want to give too much away too soon.

SOURCE 1

The home page of one of the Anne Frank websites.

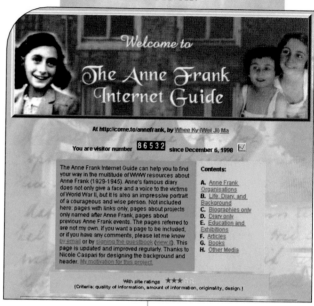

SOURCE 2

A painting of the storming of the Bastille during the French Revolution.

SOURCE 3

I say to you today, my friends, that even though we face the difficulties of today and tomorrow, I still have a dream. It is a dream deeply rooted in the American dream. I have a dream that one day this nation will rise up and live out the true meaning of its belief 'that all men are created equal.'

I have a dream that my four little children will one day live in a nation where they will not be judged by the colour of their skin but by the content of their character.

Part of Martin Luther King's 'I have a dream' speech.

SOURCE 4

The desperate act of a woman who rushed from the rails on to the course apparently so that she could spoil the race; her action was deliberate. She was ridden down by the King's horse. She is said to be in the Suffragist movement, she had 'Suffragist colours' tied around her waist. We think that yesterday's exhibition does more harm than good to the cause of votes for women.*

* Suffragist – a person who wanted women to be able to vote

This is an account from *The Times* newspaper of 5 June 1913 about the death of Emily Davison at the Derby horse race.

SOURCE 5

A photograph of the Taj Mahal in India.

SOURCE 6

A painting of the
execution of Mary,
Queen of Scots in 1587.

Den VIII february werde onthalst Maria
Stuart Schots Coninginne's teruende Roomsch Catho-

Activity Time

1 In pairs or groups, copy this chart and fill it in for one of the
sources on pages 14–18. This way you will begin to work out about
some of the topics we will study. You may recognise some already.

Source number and type	What does it show/ describe?	What might be happening? What clues does it give you?
e.g. Source 2 – painting		

2 Now swap your findings with
another group and fill in another
row on your chart.

3 a Match some of the pictures to the
four headlines below.
b Make up a headline or a more
exciting caption to go with two
more of the sources.

> **Off with her head – Queen has own cousin executed**

> **Beautiful tomb built for dead wife of Shah (ruler) as love gift**

> **Dying Emily tells the king: Give women the vote!**

> **Shock as Royal family lose their heads and France is turned upside down**

SOURCE 7

A nineteenth-century cartoon called 'A Court for King Cholera'.

FANCY A CHALLENGE?

Can you find some primary sources (sources from the time) connected to any of Sources 1-8 or from the same stories? Here are some clues to where you could look:

- School textbooks
- Encyclopaedias
- Library books
- The Internet

Here's some advice! Before you start hunting, make a list of the key words that you will look up to find some more sources. Then make a note of what your source is and where you found it. You could use a chart like this to help you with this task:

What topic am I interested in?	What key words should I look up?	What type of source have I found?	Where exactly did I find it?

4 Look at the map on pages 4 and 5. Make a list of which countries the stories in Sources 1-8 come from. What do you notice?

5 Now do the same for the timeline on pages 6 and 7. What do you notice about the time periods that Sources 1-8 come from?

6 Choose two topics that you are looking forward to investigating and explain what it is about them that interests you.

A HEALTH WARNING! PROBLEMS AND GAPS IN EVIDENCE

Historians have to be very careful not to draw the wrong conclusions from evidence or be misled by sources. Some sources may not tell us the exact truth and may not be reliable (trustworthy). Look again at Source 7. Can you think of any reason why this might not tell us the whole truth about life in London in the nineteenth century? Have you thought about what type of source it is? In order to check that sources are reliable we have to ask some questions, just like detectives and police. Here are three of the questions we might ask about a source to check that it is reliable:

- Who made/wrote the source?
- When was it made/written?
- Why was it made/written?

Remember that some sources are reliable, but often we have to be on the safe side and check. Another thing to remember is that even sources we cannot trust might tell us something important.

SOURCE 8

A reconstruction of Piltdown Man's skull found in 1912. Piltdown Man was presented as the link between modern man and his distant ancestor the ape. In 1953 Piltdown Man was shown to be a fake: the skull fragments were human and the jaw belonged to an ape.

Question Time

1. Why is it important to know who wrote or made a source before we can use it as solid evidence? Explain your answer.

2. Can you pick out a source from 1–8 that may not be telling us the exact story? Explain why you might be suspicious of it as evidence.

3. Can you think of any reasons why Source 7 could be called the odd one out? Think about what sort of people and events the other sources tell us about.

4. Can you think of any group of people from any time in history about whom it would be difficult to find any sources? Does this mean that we should not study them?

WHAT'S HISTORY GOT TO DO WITH ME?

HISTORY EXPLAINS THE PRESENT

WHAT'S GOING ON?

You must have seen or heard some news about the peace process in Northern Ireland on the television or radio recently. The problems between the Catholics and Protestants in Northern Ireland have been in the news for many years now. Do you know the full story and what the latest situation is? It is impossible to understand without history.

SOURCE 1

IRA Guns Deal Hope

General John de Chastelain has been given secret information to help save the Ulster peace process it was claimed yesterday. De Chastelain is said to have received private documents from an IRA go-between. He added that this was strong enough to bring back the power sharing ruling council that was suspended by Secretary of State for Northern Ireland, Peter Mandelson, three days ago. The papers are believed to include details of a timetable for the hand-over of terrorist guns and explosives. Northern Ireland politicians continue to blame each other for the crisis yesterday and Ulster Unionists called the secret IRA offer 'a gimmick'.

An extract from *The Mirror* newspaper, 14/2/00.

Question Time

1. What do you think a power sharing council is?

2. What new information does the article claim to know about?

3. Why do you think that this information is important?

4. Do the Ulster Unionists seem to be on the same side as the IRA?

5. a Find proof that the journalist cannot be sure about parts of the story.
   b What problems does this cause us?

Are you still a little confused about this story? It's not surprising if you are. Newspaper articles are written for day-to-day readers and do not often stop to introduce people to stories and events.

Question Time

1 Make a list of five things that this article does not explain. Make a list of five things that you still want to know having read this article.

2 You are a reporter for your school magazine covering this important news story. It is your job to research the story ready to interview an important politician who is visiting your school. You will need to know what to ask him or her and understand enough to have a conversation about the story. Make a plan and do some research ready for the big interview. Use these suggestions to help you to prepare:

a What do I need to know? (eight questions minimum)

b What sources of evidence could I use to help me to answer these questions? (at least five different sources)

c What have I found out so far?

d What am I still confused about? What can I do about it?

e What four questions would I like to ask in the interview?

f Write up your questions and how the politician might have answered in an article for the school magazine.

3 Can you remember any news stories from the past few months where you need understanding of the past to make sense of the present? Plot these events on the map on pages 4 and 5 to see where they are taking place.

4 Use the plan to find out about a story in your local newspaper. Share your findings with the rest of the class.

The plan in Question 2 can be used to help you to find out about anything – the news stories today or events in the past, and also information for your other school subjects. Remember how important it is to think and ask questions before you start to do some research.

How much of your information was about events from the past? You should now see how important it is to understand the past or what is happening in the present can become a mystery. Most events today are affected by the past in some way.

Summary

- We need history to understand what's happening today and what will make the history of the future.
- To find out about events, we have to ask questions.
- We can get answers from many different types of sources.
- We need to think and ask questions about all sorts of stories – from international news headlines to what's happening in our local area.

VISITING THE PAST

We have lots of history on our doorsteps. As we travel to school we see street names, objects and buildings that are obvious reminders of the past. Some historic buildings are lived in, some are used as places of work, while others are kept as evidence of our heritage. Organisations like the National Trust and English Heritage help to look after special historic places and use them to help people understand the past. We can use historic sites such as churches, castles, forts, factories, houses, markets, streets and pubs to investigate the past. Just as with written or visual sources, we have to examine the evidence very carefully and search for clues. Sometimes these clues are hidden. We also have to ask questions. Sometimes the buildings themselves raise many questions that are ways of finding out more about history.

VISIT NUMBER 1 – THE MIDDLE AGES

You will probably have been on a History field trip somewhere and collected evidence (sometimes called data) as part of an investigation. Here is an historic site that we can investigate. Let's visit the Middle Ages.

There are photographs below and a plan of an abbey. Remember that just by looking and asking questions we can find out a lot.

SOURCE 1

A photograph of Fountains Abbey.

On page 23 you will find an Evidence Sheet. It includes questions to help you to use the abbey building as evidence. It also contains some examples to help you. Once you have closely examined the abbey plan and the photographs, copy and fill in the sheet with as many ideas as you can. Use Source 3, the Visitors' Information Box and the Key Words Clues to help you.

SOURCE 2

An aerial photograph of Fountains Abbey.

SOURCE 3

A plan of Fountains Abbey.

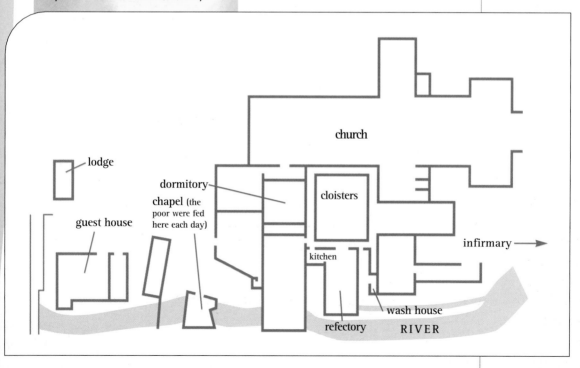

KEY WORDS CLUES

To help you fill in your Evidence Sheet think about these key words:

- Size of rooms
- Different shapes (different window shapes were in fashion at different times)
- Materials
- Gaps/holes
- What is missing?

SOURCE 4

Visitors' Information Box

Fountains Abbey is near Ripon in North Yorkshire. It is set in a valley for protection from the weather and is surrounded by good farming land, rivers and streams. It was founded (set up) in 1132 by a group of monks who wanted to escape from the normal world and concentrate on praising God. When they first arrived in the valley they probably lived in wooden huts and built a wooden church. After a few years, a huge abbey was built from stone. Buildings of stone were rare in the Middle Ages and were usually the most important buildings in an area. Fountains Abbey would have held up to 250 monks at one time. Monks lived and worked there until 1536 when Henry VIII closed down the monastery and took its wealth.

Evidence Sheet:

Look and see – asking questions

What do you notice? Describe eight things that you can see or notice.

(e.g., why is the biggest room on the left?)

What do you want to know? List at least eight questions that you would like to ask a tour guide or expert about the site, based on what you can see.

(e.g., did they have glass in the windows?)

Look back at the Visitors Information Box and Source 1. Can you have a guess at the answers to any of your questions?

(e.g., perhaps there is no glass because…)

What might confuse us about this site? Are there any problems for the historian here?

(e.g., bits might have been pulled down)

What more do we need to know/find out?

(e.g., what did the monks eat?)

What other sources would we want to look for?

(e.g., any letters from the monks?)

Conclusions:

This site tells us about:

(e.g., what was important to the monks?)

VISIT NUMBER 2 – THE NINETEENTH CENTURY

Our second example is part of the unusual village of Saltaire in Yorkshire. Fill in an Evidence Sheet again to find out all about it. This time you do not have a clues box or examples to help. Try to draw your own conclusions.

SOURCE 5

A photograph of houses at Saltaire.

Visitors' Information Box

Saltaire was a village built by a man called Sir Titus Salt. Salt owned some textile factories and wanted a perfect village to keep his workers happy. He wanted it to be different from the crowded and polluted areas of nearby Bradford. It was built between 1851 and 1872 and contained houses and other buildings as well as two huge mills.

SOURCE 6

Part of the huge mill in Saltaire. The many windows would let in light and air to the busy workrooms.

SOURCE 7

A plan of Saltaire showing the mill, workers' houses and leisure facilities.

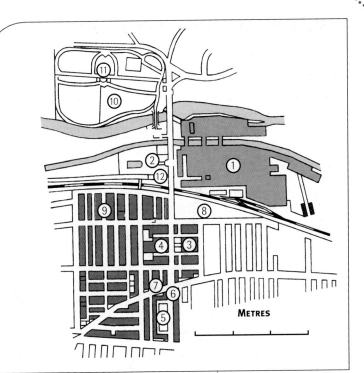

①	The Mill
②	Church
③	The Institute
④	The School
⑤	The Almshouses
⑥	The Hospital
⑦	Chapel
⑧	Sunday School
⑨	The Bath and Washhouse
⑩	The Park
⑪	Statue of Sir Titus Salt
⑫	Workers' Dining Room
▓	Workers' Houses

METRES

HISTORY CHALLENGE

Make a list of all the historic sites or buildings that you know in your local area. You can include examples like local churches, markets and other old buildings. Next to each example note down what period in the past the place is from and two things that the site could tell you about. Fill in your information on a chart with headings like this:

Place from the past	Time period/s	What can it tell us about?

Summary

In this section you have learnt that:
- There is history all around us.
- Buildings can also be used as evidence as well as other sources.
- We have to observe them carefully.
- We can ask questions about buildings and sites.
- They can help us to answer many questions about the past.

Question Time

❶ Draw a plan of your school and label it with 'This tells us...' sentences to show what sort of information it would tell a historian. One example might be the sports hall. This might tell us that children today are interested in keeping fit.

❷ Buildings and ruins can confuse and mislead historians just as much as other sources. Do you agree? Explain your answer fully.

❸ Design an pamphlet for young people to advertise either Fountains Abbey or Saltaire or a historic site near you. Include:
- Why should people visit?
- What should they look for?
- What sort of things does the site tell us about?

Unit 2: How did medieval monarchs keep control?

In this Unit you are going to find out about some of the most exciting and important events and people in British history. During this time at least three monarchs were murdered, one of them with a red hot poker. One king was so worried about being murdered that he slept with weapons under his bed. Another king fought a war against his wife and sons. At least three kings totally lost control of their kingdoms during the Middle Ages!

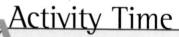

I OBEY BECAUSE IF I DON'T THEY'LL CHOP MY HEAD OFF...

We are going to use this Unit to learn about how monarchs ruled their people and their lands. At the end of the Unit you are going to answer an important question: How did medieval monarchs keep control?

Some monarchs were better at keeping control than others. Some were able to conquer new lands and control them, as well as ruling England. They were able to solve many problems to do with land, rich people, poor people, the Church, and law and order. Different monarchs used different ways to get their people to obey them and some of these ways worked better than others. Throughout history people have obeyed their rulers for different reasons.

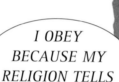

I OBEY BECAUSE MY RELIGION TELLS ME TO...

In the Middle Ages, most people obeyed their rulers for a mixture of reasons.

I OBEY BECAUSE I GET SOMETHING OUT OF IT...

I OBEY BECAUSE I KNOW MY PLACE

Activity Time

In this unit there are particular words that you need to understand.

power   control   conqueror
monarch (king/queen)   ruler
invasion   defence   attack

❶ Think about the meaning of each word. Use a dictionary if you need to. Draw a picture to communicate the meaning of three words. You must not use words in your picture.

❷ Now see if the other people in the class can work out which word you are communicating.

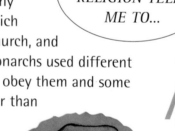

HOW DID WILLIAM OF NORMANDY TAKE CONTROL OF ENGLAND?

On 25 December 1066 a man called William was crowned King of England in Westminster Abbey in London. The man was a foreigner and the ceremony was in French, as well as English. Outside the abbey, his soldiers waited for him. They were also foreigners and could not understand everything that was going on around them. As they waited, they got nervous. What was going on inside the abbey? They could hear loud cries. Was their leader being attacked? What were the English people around them talking about? Maybe there were unfriendly English soldiers just around that corner...The soldiers became more nervous and started to set fire to some of the buildings around the abbey. 'You can't mess with us', they seemed to be saying to the local people. 'There might be fewer of us but we are here to stay...'

- How had a foreigner become King of England?
- Why were his soldiers so nervous?
- Who might be his enemies and who might be his friends?
- How would he treat the English people?

In this section you are going to find out about William, a duke from Normandy, who conquered England and became its king. William's take-over of England is called the 'Norman Conquest' because he came from Normandy in France. He is known as William the Conqueror.

GETTING AND KEEPING POWER

In order to conquer England and rule it as a king, William needed to get power and keep power.

He used different ways (strategies) to do this. Sometimes he used force and violence, and at other times he used persuasion. Most successful rulers use both of these tactics. It is difficult to rule by force alone – a lot of soldiers would be needed! Instead most rulers try to persuade the people that it is a good idea to obey them. There are many different ways this can be done. So a ruler doesn't just need to be forceful, but also clever and cunning. Your task is to look out for all the different qualities that William had which made him a successful 'conqueror'. Look out for the following qualities:

- clever and cunning ideas
- being prepared
- determination
- support from others

Question Time

1 What other qualities might a leader need? Think of leaders that are familiar to you (headteacher, prime minister), what qualities do they have?

2 William also had some good luck! As we shall see, being lucky was seen as very special in the Middle Ages. Being lucky could be a sign that God was on your side. It was very helpful for kings to have God on their side! What does this tell you about religion in the Middle Ages?

GETTING POWER

In order to find out how William got power in the first place, we need to go back in time. In December 1065, Edward 'the Confessor', King of England, lay dying. The Witan (King's Council) met to talk about a very important question. Who would become King of England after Edward's death?

There was no easy answer. Edward had no obvious heir, such as children or close relatives who could take the throne. Even if he had, it would not have been automatic because there were no rules of succession at that time.

William, Duke of Normandy had visited Edward in 1051. Later he claimed that Edward had promised that William would become king after Edward's death. Edward had grown up in Normandy and had many Normans around him in his court. William was already very powerful. The Normans were famous for their skills as soldiers and William had his own army. He had increased his power by taking over lands around Normandy but he also wanted to rule England. However, he wasn't the only one.

RIVALS FOR THE ENGLISH THRONE

Harald Hardrada Hardrada was King of Norway and already very powerful. As a descendent of King Canute, Harald claimed that he had a right to the English throne. Harald had the support of Tostig, Harold Godwinson's brother. Tostig had been banished from England and wanted to return to get back all his lands.

Harold Godwinson Harold was Earl of Wessex, a powerful English baron. His sister Edith was Edward's wife. Harold was rich, powerful and had his own army. He claimed that the king named him as his successor just before Edward's death.

The Witan knew that rulers from the continent would be more likely to invade England if it did not have a king. On the day of Edward's funeral, Harold was crowned King of England by the Witan. So in order to conquer England, William had to defeat two other rivals.

Question Time

1. Why might the Witan think that England was more likely to be invaded if it had no king?

2. Read the information about Harold Godwinson again. Can you think of any other reasons why the Witan might be in a hurry to crown Harold as king?

3. Harold must make a speech to the Witan explaining why he should be king. Write a few notes for him that show clearly why his claim to be king is better than William's or Hardrada's.

WILLIAM GETS READY

When William heard that Harold had been crowned King of England, he got ready to invade. Trees in Normandy were cut down and made into boats to cross the channel. William already had a well-trained army of knights, archers and foot soldiers. Some of William's advisers told him not to go – it would be too difficult to conquer England. But William was determined! He went around getting help from his neighbours in France. If they would help him conquer England, he told them, he would reward them with English land. By the summer, William and his army were ready. But all summer the wind blew in the wrong direction for William as he waited in Normandy with his army, so his boats could not sail.

SOURCE 1

A scene from the Bayeux Tapestry showing trees being cut down for William's boats.

INVASION IN THE NORTH OF ENGLAND

That same wind blowing from the north was able to help Harald Hardrada sail from Norway, and Tostig came with him. In the autumn of 1066 Harald Hardrada landed in north-east England. Harold had been expecting invasions from all three of his rivals, but did not know who would come first! When he heard about the arrival of Harald Hardrada and Tostig, he travelled from London with his army to meet them at Stamford Bridge and they fought a battle there on 25 September.

The battle was a great victory for King Harold and the English. Both Harald Hardrada and Tostig were killed. So many of their soldiers were killed that out of the 200 ships that had sailed to England from Norway, only 24 were needed to take the survivors back.

INVASION IN THE SOUTH OF ENGLAND

Harold was not able to celebrate for long. On the 28 September William landed in Pevensey on the south coast of England. King Harold began the long march (about 400 kilometres) back down to the south to defend his lands yet again. His soldiers and his horses were tired after the battle of Stamford Bridge and many had been killed and injured. But if he was to defend England against William he had to get to the south as quickly as possible. He did not want William to have time to get ready for a battle.

THE BATTLE

Harold took up position on top of a hill (Senlac Hill), about 14 kilometres from Hastings, and waited for William. Harold was higher up and had more men than William – between 6000 and 7000. Although William's army was smaller, most of it was better trained and it had more knights on horseback than Harold's.

On 14 October, the Battle of Hastings took place. It was a savage and brutal battle. Some of Harold's foot soldiers fought with very sharp double-handed battle-axes. Close up they were very dangerous and could cut off a man's head. So, at first, it was hard for William's soldiers to get close. At the top of the hill, Harold's soldiers used their shields to form a tight 'wall' that William's soldiers could not get through. Harold stayed behind this wall. At first it seemed as though King Harold would be victorious. William's men had to gallop uphill towards the shield 'wall', and they could not break it up.

Some of William's men became frightened and ran away down the hill. This tempted some of Harold's men to chase after them, which broke up the shield 'wall'. Then William had a good idea. Maybe they could trick King Harold's army into breaking up the shield 'wall' even more! This time some of William's soldiers pretended to run away and again Harold's men followed them. At the bottom of the hill, William's men turned and massacred Harold's soldiers. By evening Harold had very few men left at the top of the hill and William and his army were able to reach Harold and kill him.

SOURCE 2

A scene from the Bayeux Tapestry showing broken bodies on the ground.

Thousands of men had been killed and injured in the battle. Their broken bodies were scattered around Senlac Hill. After the battle an abbey was built there as a memorial to those killed.

WILLIAM MARCHES TO LONDON

William had won the Battle of Hastings, as it became known. He had defeated and killed the King of England, but, he was not yet William 'the conqueror'. First he had to be crowned king at Westminster Abbey in London. There were new dangers ahead. There might be unfriendly English soldiers waiting on the road to London. How would he get the powerful English barons to agree to his rule? Some had been killed with Harold but others, like Edwin of Mercia and Morcar of Northumbria, might not want William as king.

William marched to London, passing through important towns like Dover and Canterbury on the way. There was a castle of English soldiers at Dover which he needed to defeat. As he got near to London William heard that there were hostile (unfriendly) English soldiers on London Bridge. Therefore, William decided to come into London from the north via Wallingford, where he crossed the Thames, and then through Berkhamsted. On the way he burnt some villages and crops.

Finally at Berkhamsted Edwin, Morcar and some rulers of the Church agreed to accept William as king. He arrived at Westminster Abbey to be crowned King of England. He told everyone that he was the rightful successor to the throne. This was another good idea. It made him look less like a 'foreign conquerer' and more like the rightful successor.

William had gained power. He had invaded England, defeated Harold and been crowned king. Was this the end of William's road to power, or was it just the beginning?

Question Time

1 Make a timeline 'The Events of December 1065 to December 1066'. Think about the scale of your timeline. Will you divide it into months or weeks or days? You could use a computer to make your timeline.

2 a Find your nearest war memorial. Which war is it dedicated to?
 b What else can you learn from it about the past?
 c What different reasons might people have for a war memorial?
 d Why do you think William wanted to put a memorial at Hastings?

ILLUSTRATED MAPS

Activity Time

You are writing a double-page spread for a school textbook to explain the Norman conquest to nine-year-olds. You have been told that you have room for only 300 words and that you need a large map which you will illustrate.

1 Your design department has produced a map, but it is not very interesting. So you need to improve it. Take a piece of clean paper and copy the map.

2 Now write your account. Cover:
  • threats to King Harold from overseas
  • events of September and October 1066
  • William's route to London.

3 Go back to your map and improve it by adding arrows, labels, and short pieces of information in boxes.

A What made William a successful conqueror?

4 You need to decide what made William a successful conqueror.

  a Copy out the table below (leave room for 12 rows).

  b Read the statements beneath the table. In each case decide what qualities they show and put them into the correct column. One is done for you.

Determined	Prepared	Clever and cunning	Supported by others	Lucky
		William claimed to be the rightful king of England.		

Statements

- William got promises of support from neighbours in France.
- Morcar and Edwin agreed that William should be king.
- William took trained soldiers to England.
- William told his men to pretend to run away and break up Harold's shield 'wall'.
- William entered London from the north.
- William ignored the advice in Normandy not to invade England.
- The wind meant that William could not sail in the summer.
- William prepared food, weapons and horses in Normandy.

Read pages 29–31 again. You may be able to find more qualities that made William a successful conqueror. Add them to your table.

  c Do you think that one of the qualities (columns) is more important than the others? Why do you think this?

  d Read the following statements:

- As William travelled from Hastings to London, he burnt the surrounding countryside. This was a clever way to control the people of England.
- As William travelled from Hastings to London, he burnt the surrounding countryside. This was NOT a clever way to control the people of England.

Which statement do you agree with? You should use information from page 31 to back up your choice.

HOW DO WE KNOW ABOUT THE NORMAN CONQUEST?

THE BAYEUX TAPESTRY

Most of our evidence about the Norman Conquest and the Battle of Hastings comes from a source of information called the Bayeux Tapestry. This is a large (70 metres by 48 centimetres) piece of linen with stitches in different colours of wool. It tells the story of the Norman Conquest in a series of pictures, rather like a strip cartoon. There are 72 pictures with Latin subtitles. The pictures on pages 29 and 30 are examples from the Bayeux Tapestry.

Question Time

William is the hero of the story and most of the pictures are to do with Norman soldiers and how they fought. However, the tapestry shows many other parts of the story.

1 In pairs, focus on one picture from the Bayeux Tapestry. Describe in detail the picture you have chosen. What is happening? What do you learn from it about the Norman Conquest?

2 In your pairs, you are going to make your own cartoon strip of the Norman Conquest. Read pages 28–33 again. Choose the four most important points in the story of the Norman Conquest to illustrate in your cartoon. Which choices have other groups in the class made? Are they the same or are they different?

3 The Bayeux Tapestry tells us one version of the Norman Conquest.
Whose version does it tell us? That of:

- William?
- A Norman knight?
- Harold?
- A refugee woman?

Explain why have you chosen that person.

CONTROLLING THE LAND BY BUILDING CASTLES

Read Source 1, even if Richard was exaggerating, it was probably very frightening to move around England if you were Norman in the eleventh century. It was hard to know who might be friendly and who might not. Maps were not very accurate and you could easily get lost.

Norman barons built castles to live in, to show off their power and to protect themselves against local English people who might be unfriendly towards them. Anyone who built a castle had first to get permission from William. William also built many castles of his own and these were called 'royal castles'. He was very keen to build castles to defend his new conquest.

SOURCE 1

What were left of the conquered English lay in ambush for the hated race of Normans and murdered them secretly in woods as opportunity offered.

Richard FitzNigel, in the twelfth century.

An artist's reconstruction of a motte and bailey castle.

Question Time

❶ Read again what Richard FitzNigel said. Why might he exaggerate how much the Normans were hated?

❷ Why did Norman lords want to build castles?

❸ Before 1066 there were very few castles in England. Can you work out why?

WHAT DID THE CASTLES LOOK LIKE?

Motte and bailey castles The first castles were made of wood and earth because they needed to be put up quickly. They were called motte and bailey castles.

The motte was a high mound used as a lookout and to retreat to if the castle was attacked. It was sometimes in an open area called the bailey. The motte had a wooden tower on its top and a wooden staircase from the bailey to the motte. The bailey was used for daily living. Animals would be kept there for food. The bailey would be surrounded by a high wooden wall and sometimes a moat for extra protection.

SOURCE 2

A photo of Berkhamsted, a motte and bailey castle, showing the walls of the bailey, the motte and the moat.

What were the towers for?

Why was there a tower on top of the motte?

Why was the motte a steep hill?

Why was there a drawbridge?

Why did the motte have a wooden staircase up it?

What was the moat for?

Why were animals kept in the bailey?

Why was there a well?

Why did the bailey have a high wall around it?

Activity Time

Attackers and defenders

Divide the class into 'Attackers' and 'Defenders'.

Look carefully at the map, the drawing of the motte and bailey castle and the photo on page 34.

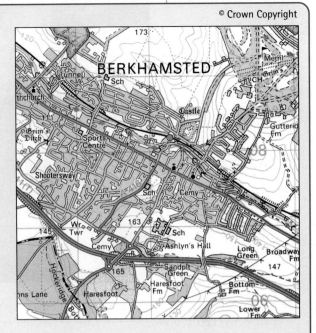
© Crown Copyright

DEFENDERS:

❶ Make a drawing of Berkhamsted Castle. Label it showing the different parts and what their purpose was. Use the questions in Source 2 to help you.

❷ What makes Berkhamsted Castle easy to defend? Make a list.

❸ How might a Norman baron, in charge of defending the castle, react? He has heard rumours that a group of hostile Englishmen is on its way to attack him.
a What plans do you think he might have made to defend the castle?
b How would he have made sure of food and water? He could have been held siege for weeks!
c How would he have defended himself if attacked with arrows, battering rams, fire, catapults?
d How would he have known when the English arrived?

ATTACKERS:

❶ Make a drawing of Berkhamsted Castle. Label it showing the different parts and what their purpose was. Use the questions in Source 2 to help you.

❷ What makes Berkhamsted Castle hard to attack? Make a list.

❸ How might an English baron, in charge of attacking the castle, react? It is 1070.
a What plans would he have made to attack the castle?
b How would he have made sure of food and water? He could have been there for weeks!
c How would he have used arrows, battering rams, fire, catapults to attack?

HOW DID STONE MAKE CASTLES STRONGER?

Towards the end of his rule, William and his barons started to use stone around the outside of castles. These were called 'shell keep' castles. Famous shell keep castles include the Castle and Tower of London's White Tower, Exeter Castle and Colchester Castle.

SOURCE 3

Colchester Castle, a shell keep castle.

Question Time

1 Look at Source 3. Why do you think this style of castle was called a 'shell keep'?

2 Why were castles using stone easier to defend than castles using wood and earth? Look at the ATTACKERS and DEFENDERS activity to give you ideas.

3 Why do you think barons had to get William's permission before building a castle?

4 Do you think there might be any disadvantages for William and other medieval kings with barons having so many castles?

CONTROLLING THE LAND AND PEOPLE BY THE FEUDAL SYSTEM

In Britain today some people are wealthier than others. In medieval times there were also richer and poorer people, but there were many differences. The division between rich and poor was much greater and there were fewer rich people and more poor people. Most people were very, very poor. Almost everyone lived off the land. Most people never used money. Instead, they grew food to eat and to swap for their other needs, such as clothes, shoes and tools.

There were also other differences from the way we live today. The king owned all the land. This was a very important way of controlling the country and its people. William was able to make this control work for him. William granted land to **barons**. This means he let them live off that land as if it were their own. But they didn't get the land for nothing; in return they promised 'military service'. They would provide knights for the king's army when he needed them. They would also fight for the king.

William granted a lot of land to the barons. For example, he gave his brother Odo 184 estates – very large areas of land with many farms on them - in Kent. Each baron granted parts of his land to **knights** who lived off that land as if it were their own. But they didn't get their land for nothing either. In return they also promised 'military service'.

The knights granted small pieces of land to **peasants**. They also had to do something in return, but it wasn't military service. In return, they farmed the land for the knight and made payments of food to the knight.

This system was called 'feudalism'. Feudal is a Latin word that describes the relationship between land and services. In return for land, you had to give service – this could mean fighting or farming.

Activity Time

Draw a diagram and label it to explain feudalism. Try it out on your classmates. Does your diagram help them?

	What they put in	What they got out
King	Land	An army of about 4000 men when he needed it.
Barons	Knights to fight in king's army. Also promised to fight.	Land
Knights	Fought for the king with the baron when needed.	Land
Peasants	Farmed the land for knights, barons and the king. Also made 'payments' of food.	Land

William did not grant all the land to others, but kept about a quarter of it for himself. He didn't just use the land to raise an army or get the barons to serve him, he also used the land to reward those who had helped him conquer England.

Feudalism solved lots of problems. It was a clever system for monarchs because it meant they could control land **and** people.

Question Time

1 Which problems did feudalism help to solve?

2 Do you think there might be any disadvantages for William and other medieval kings of the feudal system?

CONTROLLING THE LAND AND THE PEOPLE THROUGH KEEPING RECORDS

In 1085 William and his council of barons and bishops met and decided to survey all the land of England. This meant counting all land, all animals and all the people both in 1066 and in 1086. Royal officials travelled around the country asking questions and recording the answers on large rolls of parchment. Then the monks at Winchester organised this information into counties. It was the most detailed survey ever done and was called the Domesday Book because it reminded people of the story of the last judgement in the Christian religion.

WHAT DOES THE DOMESDAY BOOK HAVE TO DO WITH CONTROL?

The Domesday Book gave William a great deal of information. The following points of information would have been useful in controlling England:

- Knowing how much land and how many animals each person had was important for collecting taxes. William had collected taxes before 1086, but he did not know how wealthy people really were or who lived where!
- Knowing how land had become poorer or richer between 1066 and 1086 was important for collecting taxes.
- Knowing how many people there were was important for collecting taxes.
- Knowing who had the land before and after the conquest gave William useful information about changes during his reign. He knew which lands were empty or granted to dead or absent barons and therefore could be given to someone else.

The Domesday Book was not just useful for William, it is also very useful for historians today.

Activity Time

1 Read what each of the historians wants to find out about. One of them has made a big mistake and the Domesday Book will not help. Which one has made a mistake?

2 Explain how the Domesday Book could help each of the other three historians to answer their big questions.

3 What other historical questions could the Domesday Book help to answer?

I want to find out how poor people were in the past.

I want to find out what houses were made out of in the past.

I want to find out how many people lived in England in the past.

I want to find out how damaged England had been by the Norman Conquest.

The Domesday Book can also be used to find out about changes in the ruling class after the Norman Conquest. Historians have used it to count the number of foreign knights. In 1086 there were about 2000 out of a total population of 1.5 million. By 1086 all the barons were Norman. Therefore, at this time England was ruled by a very small and very rich 'foreign' ruling class.

Activity Time

Information is power!

1 Read the two statements below and decide which statement you agree with most.

The Domesday Book shows us that William had very good control of England. It could not have been written if he had not.

The Domesday Book shows us that William did not have good control of England. It would not have been needed if he had.

2 Can you think of anything else you have found out about William which you could use to support your chosen statement?

HOW DID A SUCCESSFUL MONARCH KEEP CONTROL?

WHY WAS WILLIAM SUCCESSFUL IN CONTROLLING THE BARONS?

Barons were the most powerful Englishmen. There were only about twelve of them but they were very rich and they had their own armies. Edward had problems with the barons. Some of them had rebelled against Edward and it seemed likely that they would rebel against William.

First, William needed to reward Norman and French barons with the land of English barons who had been killed or run away. Also he needed to defeat any rebellious barons. This would send a strong message to anyone else who might be thinking about rebelling against him.

William appointed Normans as his main advisers and gave them English lands. Bishop Odo, his half-brother, became Earl of Kent, while William FitzOsbern became Earl of Hereford.

I'm not going to become 'conqueror' overnight. I need 'staying power'!

William let English nobles who promised to serve him, keep their lands. He invited the chief English lords to stay in his court where he could keep an eye on them. It was an invitation they couldn't refuse!

Activity Time

❶ Write a letter from William to his brother, Odo. Tell him about the gift of land and why you have done it. Tell him what other actions you have taken with the English barons and why.

❷ What might Odo have said in reply? Remember he might have thought William's treatment of the barons would not work, and he would want to warn him of dangers.

HOW SUCCESSFUL WAS WILLIAM IN CONTROLLING THE BARONS?

In 1069 the barons Edwin and Morcar in the north of England rebelled against William's rule. These were the two barons who had promised to serve William at Berkhamsted, but when William tried to get taxes from them, they changed their minds. At the same time 200 Danish ships sailed up the Humber and joined the rebels. This was a rebellion and a foreign invasion at the same time! York was ransacked and the Normans who had settled there were murdered or driven out. William went north with his army and defeated the rebel English barons and the Danes.

William then travelled around Yorkshire with his army. They burnt the land, slaughtered the animals and destroyed all the tools. It was winter and the peasants had no food left and no way to grow more food. Thousands starved to death. It was called the 'Harrying (destroying) of the North'. It took the north hundreds of years to recover from this destruction.

At the time of the 'harrying' a medieval chronicler, Oderic Vitalis, wrote about the terror and destruction (see Source 1). Oderic's mother was English while his father was French. As you read the extract, think about how Oderic's own background might have influenced his reaction to the 'harrying'.

SOURCE 1

In his anger at the English barons, William commanded that all crops and herds, chattels and food should be burned to ashes, so that the whole of the north be stripped of all means of survival. So terrible a famine fell upon the people, that more than 100,000 young and old starved to death. My writings have often praised William, but for this act I can only condemn him.

Oderic Vitalis writing at the time of the harrying about the events that took place.

WILLIAM CHANGES THE WAY HE TREATS THE BARONS!

In 1066 when William was crowned king, he had allowed some English barons to keep their lands, but after 1070 this changed. By 1086 there were no English barons left – they were all Norman.

Question Time

1. Why were the barons more likely to rebel against William than against Edward the Confessor?

2. One reason for the 'Harrying of the North' was to discourage further attacks by Danes or Norwegians on northern England. Why did William think this would work?

3. What other reasons might William have had for the 'Harrying of the North'?

4. Why do you think William changed the way he treated the barons?

5. After 1070 there were very few rebellions and from 1073 onwards William spent most of his time in Normandy. What does this tell you about William's control over the barons between:
   a 1066 and 1070?
   b after 1070?

6. How did William control England?
   - What were the problems and challenges?
   - What did William do to solve the problem?
   - How good was his solution?
   - Were there any disadvantages?

HOW SUCCESSFUL WERE ENGLISH MONARCHS IN CONTROLLING THE BOUNDARIES OF ENGLAND AND THE EMPIRE?

Did any monarch make the empire bigger? How?

GETTING CONTROL OF WALES, SCOTLAND AND IRELAND

In 1200, England did not have full control of Wales, Scotland or Ireland. English monarchs wanted to rule these areas for many reasons. The larger their kingdom was, the more powerful and rich they would become. Feudalism could be introduced into all lands ruled by England. This would increase the military power of the English monarch. It also meant that they had more land to tax and more land to tax meant more money.

Ruling Scotland, Ireland and Wales was also important for strategic reasons. The position of these countries could threaten England if they were out of control. There were many raids across the borders into England, especially from Scotland. Foreign invaders could use these countries as a stepping stone to get closer to England.

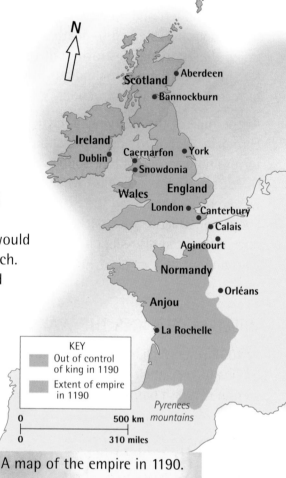

A map of the empire in 1190.

KEEPING CONTROL OF THE EMPIRE

As you can see from the map above, English monarchs had a large empire to control. Controlling the empire was a big challenge for medieval monarchs as travel was difficult, and that made it hard to rule the empire. Foreign monarchs, especially the French, were always a threat. English monarchs had to defend the empire against them and that cost money as well as taking up a large amount of time.

Question Time

❶ Look at the map and read the information above. Why do you think English monarchs wanted to keep the empire?

❷ Why was it difficult to do this?

❸ Why did English monarchs want to control Wales, Scotland and Ireland?

❹ Look very carefully at the map. Why might it be harder to conquer and control Scotland and Ireland than Wales?

THE UPS AND DOWNS OF CONTROLLING THE BORDERS: WALES, SCOTLAND, IRELAND

As you find out what happened between England and its neighbours, think about these questions: Was this event an up or a down for medieval English monarchs? An 'up' could mean that England became safer, richer, or more powerful. A 'down' could mean that England became in danger from attack, poorer, less powerful.

You are now going to look for patterns of 'ups' and 'downs' in how good medieval monarchs were at keeping control of the land around England, including the empire.

Activity Time

Draw a timeline like the one shown here. You will need at least 10 cm for each century and at least 10 cm both above and below your line. (You could make one large timeline as a group or class instead of, or as well as, your own timeline.)

For each event, decide whether it is an 'up' or a 'down and add it to your timeline.

1086 NEWS FLASH FROM WALES!
Wales is not conquered by William in the same way as England was. Norman lords settle along the border between Wales and England and some settle in southern and eastern Wales where the land is fertile but the north and west are left alone. William tries a few times to take over north and west Wales using military force, but these attempts always fail.

1260 NEWS FLASH FROM WALES!
Llywelyn ap Gruffyd (1240–82), ruler of Gwynedd, is really powerful. All the Welsh princes have agreed to obey him.

1272 NEWS FLASH FROM WALES!
Llywelyn refuses to pay homage to Edward I when he takes over as king. He had paid homage to Edward's father, Henry III!

1276 NEWS FLASH FROM WALES!
Edward is very angry. He marches into Wales and goes to war against Llywelyn.

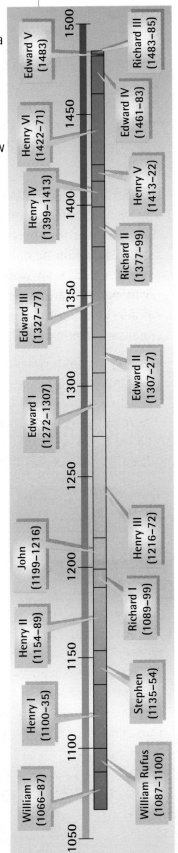

Activity Time

1282 NEWS FLASH FROM WALES!

Llywelyn and other Welsh leaders are killed. Llywelyn's castles are filled with English soldiers.

1284 NEWS FLASH FROM WALES!

To keep Wales under control, Edward:
- *makes his son Prince of Wales*
- *divides Wales into counties under English law and government*
- *builds seven castles.*

NEWS FLASH FROM WALES!

The year is 1399. A Welshman called Owain Glyndwr says that he is the Prince of Wales. He leads a rebellion against the English. He takes over many of the castles in Wales. He also makes friends with the French. In 1405, 2600 French soldiers land on the coast of Wales. They have come to help Owain Glyndwr!

❶ What does the French landing tell you about the importance to English monarchs of controlling Wales?

NEWS FLASH FROM WALES!

The English fight back. It is 1408. The English recapture castles at Harlech and Aberystwyth. The rebellion of Owain Glyndwr comes to an end. England has got back its control of Wales.

SOURCE 1

A picture of Caerphilly Castle, a concentric castle built by Edward I.

Question Time

The castle shown in Source 1 was built by Edward I to defend Wales. It is called a concentric castle.

❶ Why is it called concentric?

❷ Concentric castles were easier to defend than both a motte and bailey and a shell keep castle. Look carefully at the picture and explain why they were easier to defend.

Activity Time

NEWS FLASH FROM IRELAND!

It is the 1160s. Henry II's knight 'Strongbow' invades Ireland and makes most of the local Irish kings swear homage to Henry. Henry introduces English laws and customs, instead of Gaelic ones. English families are sent over to settle the most fertile parts of Ireland. This means forcing Irish people off the land. Some Irish lords are not happy and fight back.

❷ Why do you think Henry II introduced English laws and customs into Ireland?

Activity Time

NEWS FLASH FROM IRELAND!

Ireland is out of control. Richard II goes on two expeditions to try to get full control of Ireland. The expeditions cost a lot of money and both fail.

1500 NEWS FLASH FROM IRELAND!

Most of Ireland is still out of English control. There are over 60 Irish lords, all independent of the English monarch. By 1500, the English monarchs control only the 'Englishry' around Dublin, Meath, Kildare, Louth. They build castles, forts and ditches to protect the 'Englishry'.

1286 NEWS FLASH FROM SCOTLAND!

Scotland is free of English rule. Norman lords who settled in Scotland have become Scottish. They support the Scottish monarchs.

NEWS FLASH FROM SCOTLAND!

In 1292 the Scottish king, John Balliol, refuses to pay homage to Edward I. Edward tries to conquer all of Scotland. His cavalry fight well and he is successful.

NEWS FLASH FROM SCOTLAND!

Edward I is finding it hard to keep control of Scotland. William Wallace is fighting back and encouraging other Scots to do the same. He is only a humble knight but he gets lots of support. In 1305 he is captured and executed.

❸ Look at the map on page 42. Why did Edward I find it hard to keep control of Scotland?

1306 NEWS FLASH FROM SCOTLAND!

Robert Bruce is crowned King of Scotland. Like Wallace, he does not want to obey the English. He is a very clever soldier who uses guerrilla tactics as he has far fewer men. Instead of fighting battles, his soldiers ambush English soldiers and destroy crops so that the English cannot find food to eat. The English are forced to retreat from Scotland.

❹ Why do you think guerrilla tactics were so successful?

NEWS FLASH FROM SCOTLAND!

It is 1314 and the English refuse to give up. Edward II sends 25,000 English soldiers to fight 7000 Scots. The Scots win at the Battle of Bannockburn. The battle is very bloody, and many people die.

NEWS FLASH FROM SCOTLAND!

In 1328 Edward III accepts Bruce as king. The border between Scotland and England becomes a trouble spot. Raiders from both sides cross to steal cattle and murder each other!

Question Time

❶ Look at your timeline. Did the control of English monarchs over the borders of their neighbours increase or decrease in:
   a 1200?   b 1300?   c 1400?   d 1500?

❷ What do the events described above tell you about the relationship between land and conquest? For example, what type of land is more likely to be conquered? What type of land is less likely to be conquered?

Activity Time

THE UPS AND DOWNS OF CONTROLLING THE EMPIRE

As you read the events below, add them to your timeline.

1154 NEWS FLASH FROM THE EMPIRE!

Henry II controls a huge empire stretching from Calais in the north of France to the Pyrenees in the south. He got hold of the empire through a mixture of inheritance, conquest and marriage.

NEWS FLASH FROM THE EMPIRE!

John loses the whole of Normandy to Philip II of France in 1204.

1216 NEWS FLASH FROM THE EMPIRE!

Things are going from bad to worse. Prince Louis of France invades England to claim the English throne for himself. John dies and it is up to the Earl of Pembroke to defeat Louis.

1294 NEWS FLASH FROM THE EMPIRE!

Edward I upsets the French when he refuses to go to an important meeting in Paris. He tries to build up a big alliance of powerful rulers against the French but it does little good. Edward I is too busy trying to hold on to Wales and Scotland as well. However, Flanders and Gascony are still under his control.

1340 NEWS FLASH FROM THE EMPIRE!

Edward III claims the French throne for himself (his mother Isabella was the daughter of a French king). The fighting starts and the English have successes at the battles of Crécy and of Poitiers.

1360 NEWS FLASH FROM THE EMPIRE!

The English are winning. Under the Treaty of Bretigny, Edward III gets control of one-third of France.

1377 NEWS FLASH FROM THE EMPIRE!

Things are going downhill fast for the English. The French raid the English coast and do lots of damage.

NEWS FLASH FROM THE EMPIRE!

English luck changes under Henry V. The French King is mentally ill and the French nobles start to quarrel with each other. One of the French nobles, the Duke of Burgundy, goes over to the English side. Henry V takes advantage and in 1415 wins a great victory at Agincourt.

NEWS FLASH FROM THE EMPIRE!

Henry V follows up his victory by taking over the north of France. By the Treaty of Troyes in 1420, he controls half of France.

1428 NEWS FLASH FROM THE EMPIRE!

The English try to take the south of France too. They begin by besieging Orléans.

NEWS FLASH FROM THE EMPIRE!

Things are looking very bad for the French when a young girl called Joan of Arc tells the French king that she can help him. She claims to have God on her side. Joan of Arc wins a great victory against the English at Orléans.

1435 NEWS FLASH FROM THE EMPIRE!

Joan is captured and killed but it does no good. The Duke of Burgundy changes sides again! It is not looking good for the English.

1453 NEWS FLASH FROM THE EMPIRE!

The 'Hundred Years War' is finished. The English lose all their French lands except Calais. The empire is gone.

Question Time

1 Study your timeline again. Which medieval English monarch had the most power and control over the boundaries? Give reasons for your choice.

2 Which medieval English monarch had the least power and control over the boundaries? Give reasons for your choice.

3 Read the events again. Explain how each of the following could help monarchs get greater power and control over foreign lands:

luck   money   marriage   alliances   trouble in France

4 What factors did not help monarchs get greater power and control over foreign lands?

HOW DID MEDIEVAL MONARCHS USE LAW AND ORDER AS AN INSTRUMENT OF CONTROL?

A PUNISHMENT TO FIT THE CRIME? FINDING OUT ABOUT MEDIEVAL LAW AND ORDER.

It's market day in Richmond. Cheese, cloth, tools, ribbons are all being bought and sold. People are selling cattle, horses and sheep. Above the noise of the market, a quarrel can be heard. Two men are arguing over the price of a foal. 'It's too much,' says Edgar. 'I'm giving it away!' retorts Will. With much muttering, Edgar pays for the foal. He stands back and looks the foal over. 'Wait,' he shouts at Will, 'this foal is mine.' Will looks puzzled, 'I know it's yours, you just paid for it.' 'No! It was a foal stolen from me some weeks ago. I recognise it now.' He turns to the people who have stopped to listen to the quarrel, 'Thief!' he shouts, pointing at Will, 'This man is a thief!'

The story above really happened though the conversation has been made up. We know it happened because an historian has researched court records from England in the 1170s.

What happened next?

Edgar, who was described by a witness as a 'tall, strong and brawny' man, apparently said these exact words: 'The foal is mine, how come you have him? If you deny it, the strength of my body and power, and the power of Justice will convict you as liar.'

His words express the most important idea about crime and justice in the Middle Ages – that God would be on the side of the innocent. But how would people know whose side God was on? Do you have any ideas?

The accused man, Will, now had to stand trial. There was no police force to arrest him. But he had been accused of a crime in front of his community. According to witnesses, he was much smaller and weaker than Edgar. When Edgar accused him, he called on the blessed Saint Thomas Becket to help him prove his innocence.

A fight was organised between the two men. They would joust until there was a winner. The winner would have God on his side, and would be innocent! This fight to prove innocence was known as an 'ordeal' by people in the Middle Ages. Who do you think won the ordeal? Why do you think this?

What happened next?

Will was given three days to get ready for the ordeal. He returned home and practised jousting with his brother. When the fight happened, Will won! According to medieval beliefs, God was on his side and he was innocent.

And what about Edgar?

Look back at Edgar's words. People in the Middle Ages had a word for these words that called on God to prove innocence. They called it an oath. Both Will and Edgar had made oaths and so one must be lying! According to medieval thinking, it had to be Edgar who was lying. He confessed, and was fined. What did medieval people mean by 'oath'? What did medieval people mean by 'ordeal'?

This story doesn't just tell us what happened in Richmond in the 1170s, it also tells us how medieval people thought. Read the story again. Make a list of all the things you learn about medieval thinking.

Henry II wanted more control over law and order!

Later in this Unit you'll read about Henry II's quarrel with his friend Thomas Becket. The quarrel was about power and control over the church. Henry II also wanted more power and control over all aspects of law and order.

If you committed a crime in the twelfth century, there were three different courts where you could be put on trial.

MANOR COURT	CHURCH COURT	ROYAL COURT
Under control of barons. Barons took the money paid in fines and the land of those who were executed. Some barons were very greedy!	Under control of church. Priests were tried in church courts and they got lighter sentences than in royal court. Some priests got away with murder!	

The royal court was under the control of the monarch. Henry II wanted all serious crimes to be tried in the royal court and not in the manor or church courts.

He also wanted to make the system fairer and stronger. He ruled a large empire, and could not be everywhere at once so he needed a strong system to keep order. Henry began a new system: travelling judges were sent around the country to judge cases. This was called the assize system. Before the travelling judges arrived, juries of local men were gathered together. They decided who would be accused of crimes as there were no police to charge and arrest people.

Question Time

❶ Copy the table on page 48. Complete it to show what the royal court did and who controlled it.

❷ How did Henry II change the system of law and order?

❸ Why did Henry want to change the system of law and order? Think about power and control, money and justice.

❹ The juries had to be local men who knew the background of each court case. Why do you think medieval people thought this was a good system? Would it work today? Why/why not?

Being judge and jury

Below are two different crimes, and their punishments, from the Middle Ages.

A. Robert is guilty of poaching a deer from the royal forest. This is a very serious offence because it is against royal property. He is executed by hanging. Robert is 12 years old. From this age, 'children' are punished in the same way as adults.

B. Henry of Gelly is guilty of stealing his neighbour's pig. This is quite serious because it is against property and his arm is cut off.

❺ What does 'B' tell you about medieval thinking?

❻ What does 'A' tell you about medieval thinking?

❼ What does the difference between the punishment for 'A' and for 'B' tell you about medieval thinking?

CHURCH OR STATE – WHO WAS IN CONTROL?

WHY DID THOMAS BECKET DIE?

In 1174 Henry II walked barefoot through the cathedral city of Canterbury. As he walked, 80 monks flogged his back with branches and that night he slept in a monk's cell.

We are going to use different stories from the Middle Ages to help answer the question: **How did medieval monarchs keep control?**

The story of Henry II and Becket tells us a great deal about struggles for control in the Middle Ages. You are going to be given a number of different accounts and then asked to use the information **only** in that account to explain why Becket died.

SOURCE 1

A painting from about 1200 showing the murder of Thomas Becket.

SOURCE 2

December 1170: Becket dead!

According to an eyewitness, a monk called Edward Grim, this is what happened in the cathedral that day:

The murderers came in full armour, with swords and axes...In a spirit of mad fury the knights called out 'Where is Thomas Becket, traitor to the king and to the country?' At this he quite unafraid came down the steps and answered, 'Here I am'...

'You shall die this instant', they cried.

Becket inclined his head as one in prayer and joined his hands together and uplifted them. The wicked knight leapt suddenly upon him and wounded him in the head.

Next he received a second blow on the head, but still he stood firm.

At the third blow he fell on his knees and elbows, saying in a low voice, 'For the name of Jesus I am ready to die.'

The next blow separated the crown of his head and the blood white with the brain and the brain red with the blood stained the floor. The fourth knight warded off any who sought to interfere. A fifth man placed his foot on the neck of the holy priest and scattered the brains and blood about the pavement.

Question Time

Using Source 2, write one or more sentences answering the question 'Why did Becket die?'

SOURCE 3

1170 July – December: going back in time

In 1170 Henry II was very angry when he heard that Becket had broken a promise made to him. Becket had promised Henry that he would obey Henry rather than the Pope, but in 1170 he broke his promise. Becket expelled (excommunicated) all the Church bishops who supported Henry. Being excommunicated was very serious because it meant that you could not take mass and would go to hell. Becket also asked the Pope to punish the Archbishop of York. The Archbishop of York also supported Henry.

Henry was so angry when he heard this that he shouted out: 'Who will rid me of this troublesome priest?' Some of Henry's knights heard what he said and went off to kill Becket. When Henry realised the knights had gone, he tried to stop them but it was too late.

Question Time

Using only Sources 2 and 3, write one or more sentences that answer the question 'Why did Becket die?'

SOURCE 4

1164–70: rewinding the story

As Archbishop of Canterbury, Becket did not behave as Henry had hoped; instead of supporting Henry over the Pope, he supported the Pope over Henry!

When Henry passed a law saying that all serious crimes should be tried in the King's court and not in the Church court, Becket did not back him up. Henry wanted to have more control over the Church courts.

Becket did something else that made Henry very angry. He excommunicated barons from the Church without asking the permission of the king. This made Henry angry because he wanted to have control over the Church.

In 1170 Henry II asked the Archbishop of York to crown his son as the future king. Traditionally the Archbishop of Canterbury did this and therefore it was an insult to Becket to ask someone else. Henry seemed to be saying that he had no respect for Becket and did not need his support any more.

Question Time

Using Sources 2–4, write one or more sentences that answer the question 'Why did Becket die?'

SOURCE 5

1154–64: back to the beginning

In 1154 Henry became King of England. He asked his friend Thomas Becket to be his adviser and at first the two men worked well together.

Henry wanted to increase his power over the Church. He wanted to control the Church in England, instead of the control being with the Pope. He wanted to appoint his own men to be bishops in the Church, although the Pope was supposed to do this. He also wanted to increase his power over the clergy (priests and bishops) by controlling their system of justice. When Henry became king, clergy who were accused of committing serious crimes (like murder) did not have to be tried in the royal courts like everyone else, but could be tried in Church courts instead. These Church courts did not give such stiff sentences and some clergy got away with murder! Henry wanted to stop this happening.

In 1162 he made Becket Archbishop of Canterbury. He thought Becket would help him.

Question Time

❶ Using all the sources, write one or more sentences answering the question 'Why did Becket die?'

❷ Look at your list of causes for the death of Becket.
a As the story of Henry II and Becket moves back in time does it have more or less to do with their personal quarrel?
b As the story of Henry II and Becket moves back in time does it have more or less to do with a power struggle between King and Church?

BEFORE THE BIRTH OF HENRY II OR BECKET

In the Middle Ages the Roman Catholic Church was very important in people's lives. Most people believed that God controlled everything. For example, wars, sickness, weather, were all controlled by God. Every village had a church and everyone would go to church on Sunday to take mass. If they didn't take mass, they would go to hell after their death.

The head of the Church was not the king but the Pope in Rome. However, many medieval kings did not accept this. They felt threatened by the power of the Pope and struggled to control the Church themselves. Henry I, grandfather of Henry II, had also tried to control the Church by appointing his own men as bishops.

The death of Becket was not just about a quarrel between two men, it was also about the struggle of Henry II to control the Church. This struggle went back further in time than either Henry II or Becket. We can say that some of the causes of Becket's death went back even before his birth or the birth of Henry II.

Now write one or more sentences that answer the question 'Why did Becket die?'

WHY DID BECKET DIE?

Two historians have studied the death of Becket and are arguing about the reasons for it.

- Becket died because of a personal quarrel between himself and Henry II. The two men had been friends, but from 1163 to 1170 they fell out. They tried to patch up the quarrel but it didn't work. So when Henry got really angry he told his knights to kill Becket.

- Becket died because of a power struggle over the Church. It was nothing to do with whether they liked each other. As ruler of the country, Henry II thought that he and not the Pope in Rome should control the English Church. He was very determined because the Church was so important in medieval times.

Question Time

❶ Take each explanation and see how much evidence you can find to support it.

❷ Which of the above is the 'better' answer for someone learning about control and power in the Middle Ages?

WHAT HAPPENED WHEN MONARCHS LOST CONTROL?

KING JOHN GIVES UP SOME POWER

Not all medieval kings were as good at keeping control as William.

THE KING RETREATS

In June 1215, King John had to flee from London. The barons were marching south to see John and they were very angry about the way he was treating them. John ran for safety to Windsor Castle. He knew that he could not defeat the barons and so he agreed to meet them.

SOURCE 1

A picture of King John taken from a fourteenth-century manuscript.

On 15 June a meeting took place between the king and the barons in a meadow called Runnymede, near the River Thames. At this meeting King John had to agree to the demands made by the barons. These were written down and called Magna Carta or Great Charter. They were a set of rules that John would have to obey. A committee of 25 barons was set up to make sure John kept to the rules. This was the first time that a king was forced to obey rules. King John had lost control.

KING JOHN AND THE BARONS

In order to understand the story of King John and the barons we need to go further back to the reign of Richard I. (Look back at the timeline on page 43 to find out when this was.). Richard I was a great fighter and built a great castle at Château Gaillard in France to defend his land in Normandy. However, the castle cost a lot of money to build and Richard's crusades in the east had also been expensive. When King John came to the throne in 1199, he needed to raise more taxes than Richard had done.

All monarchs before John had asked for taxes from the people but John asked for more than many monarchs before him. Under the feudal system, kings could ask their barons and knights to fight for them when needed. They could also ask for 'scutage'. Scutage was money given to the king instead of military service. Richard I and Henry II had also asked for scutage but John asked for it more often and he increased the amount to be paid. However, scutage was not the only way John got money. When a baron died, his son had to pay 'relief' money before he could take over the land. John asked for larger amounts of 'relief' money than other kings before him.

The barons did not like paying out more money and some refused to pay. As a result, John punished them by hanging their sons. John lost the respect of some of the barons when he did this.

He had other problems, too. In 1204 the French king, Philip II, invaded and conquered Normandy. This made John look weak in the eyes of the barons, especially when they compared him to Richard I. In 1214 John tried to get back Normandy and other lands lost to the French. But it was all a failure. John came back to England still short of money, and still the loser in France.

Like his father Henry II, John also struggled to control the Church. In 1206 he quarrelled with the Pope over who should choose the next Archbishop of Canterbury. Neither John nor the Pope would give in and the Pope was so angry that he banned all Church services in

England. This was a terrible thing for the English people. They could not be christened, receive mass or a Christian burial. In 1213 John gave in to the Pope and the ban was lifted.

In 1216, a year after signing Magna Carta, John died with little money and the French in occupation of London.

Question Time

1 What did medieval monarchs grant to their barons in return for military service?

2 Why did John need money?

3 Why would a ban on church services be so terrible?

4 Make a plan of how you could answer the question: Why did John argue with the barons?
 • Read again the section above and make a list of paragraph headings.
For example,
Paragraph 1: John did not seem as successful as his brother, Richard.
Paragraph 2: John upset the barons over money.
 • What headings could you use for the other paragraphs?
 • Make notes under each paragraph heading. What information will you choose to explain why John argued with the barons?

The main points of the Magna Carta

• *The amount of tax would be fixed. Taxes could not be increased without the permission of the barons and the bishops.*

• *All freemen had a right to a fair trial with a jury. They could not be put in prison without a fair trial.*

• *The king could not interfere with the Church by appointing his own men to be bishops or archbishops.*

• *Barons had to pay only £100 to inherit land not the much larger sums John had asked for.*

Magna Carta was written by barons to protect themselves. Its terms applied only to freemen. At the time that Magna Carta was agreed, very few people were freemen, most were villeins or unfree. Over time, however, more and more people became free and Magna Carta became more and more important. Two of the points made in Magna Carta still apply today.

Question Time

1 Which two points of Magna Carta are still important today?

2 Why do you think the other two points shown above (there were 63 points in total) are not important today?

3 Magna Carta was important because it was used later to protect the rights of the people against the monarch. It became one way of protecting the freedom of people against the power of the monarch.

Explain how Magna Carta meant that medieval monarchs had lost some power.

HOW POWERFUL A KING WAS JOHN?

Some historians have argued that John was a very bad king. They point out that:

- In 1213 John gave up some power to the Pope.
- In 1214 John was defeated by Philip Augustus of France.
- In 1215 John was forced to sign Magna Carta.
- In 1216 John died with little money and the French in occupation of London.

Activity Time

Let us use the evidence that we have to reach a conclusion. Find a partner, and agree that one of you will use Evidence Group A and one Evidence Group B.

As you read, collect notes that might help to answer the question: **How bad a king was John?**

Evidence Group A

SOURCE 1

Foul as it is, Hell itself is made more horrible by the foulness of King John.

Matthew Paris writing in the thirteenth century.

SOURCE 2

John was a tyrant, a destroyer who crushed his own people. He lost Normandy and many other lands. He hated his wife and gave orders that her lovers should be strangled on her bed.

Matthew Paris, writing in the thirteenth century.

SOURCE 4

In 1209, Geoffrey, a priest, said it was not safe for priests to work for John. John heard about this and, in a temper, had Geoffrey put in prison, dressed in a cope of lead and starved to death.

Roger of Wendover, writing in the thirteenth century.

SOURCE 3

John – the very worst of all our kings. a faithless son, a treacherous brother polluted with every crime...broke every promise...

Quoted in Stubbs's *Constitutional History* in 1875.

Evidence Group B

SOURCE 1

John made sure that justice was being done in the courts. He made sure that mercy was given to widows, orphans and poor people who had done wrong.

An extract from a history textbook written in the 1960s.

SOURCE 2

John was generous and gave freely to outsiders...He trusted English people less than he trusted foreigners, so they abandoned him before the end.

From the *Barnwell Chronicle*.

SOURCE 3

We commit the Jews living in your city to your charge. If anyone tries to harm them, always protect and help them.

John's orders to an English city.

Question Time

1 Write a paragraph using the information from your Evidence Group to answer the question 'How bad a king was John?'

2 Now compare your answer with your partner's.

3 Why do you think they are different?

4 What do you learn about the job of the historian from this exercise?

Knowing about the authors

In order to understand more about why there are different views of King John, we need to know more about the authors.

5 Look at Source 3 in Evidence Group A. When did Stubbs publish his ideas about King John?

6 Look at Sources 1, 2 and 4 in Evidence Group A. When did Matthew Paris and Roger of Wendover write down their ideas about King John?

7 Stubbs based his book on the evidence of Matthew Paris and Roger of Wendover. How does this help us to understand what Stubbs says about John?

8 Matthew Paris and Roger of Wendover were both monks. How might the events of 1206–13 help us to understand why they did not like King John?

In the twentieth century, historians discovered that Geoffrey was still alive after John's death so either the Geoffrey in Source 4 was someone else or Wendover was lying. This shows that you cannot always trust what people say. Historians have to check everything against other sources of information.

SOURCE 4

John was well educated, intelligent and very active in governing his kingdom. In these ways John was a better ruler than his brother, Richard I, who neglected the kingdom. But Richard was admired for his successes on the battlefield whereas John suffered heavy defeats. In the Middle Ages it was difficult for a king to gain respect if he failed as a warrior.

An extract from a modern history textbook.

CONTROLLING THE SUCCESSION: COULD WOMEN RULE?

Look at the rulers on the timeline on page 43. It shows all the monarchs of England between 1066 and 1500. They are all men! Can you think of any reason why a woman could not rule a country as well as a man?

In the Middle Ages, people could certainly think of reasons. They had different ideas about women compared with our ideas today.

WHO WAS MATILDA?

Matilda was the daughter of Henry I. She had been brought up in the royal family. She understood the kind of behaviour that was needed to be powerful. At the age of eight, she was sent to Germany to marry a future German emperor. Her marriage to Henry V, Holy Roman Emperor, in 1114 at the age of twelve, was designed to make England and her own royal family even more powerful. But Matilda's husband died, and in 1128, when Matilda was 24 years old, she was married again. This time she was against the marriage, but her father ordered her to go through with it. What do you learn from Matilda's story about royal marriages in medieval times? What did royal marriage have to do with power and control?

One night in 1120, something happened that changed Matilda's life for ever. A boat called *The White Ship* hit a rock and sank as it crossed the channel from Normandy to England. On board the ship was Matilda's brother, son of Henry I and heir to the English throne.

The big question now was: Who would rule England after the death of Henry I? Both Matilda and a man called Stephen felt that they had a claim.

STEPHEN'S CLAIM

Stephen was the nephew of Henry I and cousin to Matilda. He had the support of some powerful barons. What claim did Matilda have?

SOURCE 1

A picture of Matilda from a medieval manuscript.

SOURCE 2

Matilda sent for the richest men and demanded from them a huge sum of money, not with gentleness, but with the voice of authority. They complained that they did not have any money left because of the war. When the people said this, Matilda, with a grim look, her forehead wrinkled into a frown, every trace of a woman's gentleness removed from her face, blazed into unbearable fury.

From *Gesta Stephani*. The author wrote this book at the time to make people support Stephen over Matilda.

WHAT HAPPENED NEXT?

Henry decided to leave the crown to his daughter, Matilda. All the barons were made to promise that they would accept Matilda as queen. Some kept their promise but others did not and instead took Stephen's side. Some barons saw the civil war which followed as a chance to increase their power. They took advantage of the troubles to do things that had not been allowed in the past, such as building big castles without getting the permission of the king.

In 1141 Matilda defeated Stephen and ruled alone. Many barons and many Londoners fought against her. But in the following year Stephen escaped and the fighting started again. This time Matilda gave up but made Stephen promise that her son Henry would succeed him.

A WOMAN'S PLACE IN MEDIEVAL SOCIETY

What do we learn from Matilda's story about a woman's place in medieval society? Sources 2 and 3 were both written during the twelfth century. They describe the events of 1141 when Matilda captured Stephen and ruled England for a very short time. As you read them, take notes of any clues about how people thought about women in medieval times.

SOURCE 3

Just about this time (1141) Stephen's wife, a woman with the determination of a man, sent messengers to Matilda. The messengers asked Matilda to free Stephen from his filthy dungeon...But Matilda abused them in harsh and insulting language.

The people of London were in big trouble now. Their land was being destroyed by the war. It was only fit to feed a hedgehog now. There was no one ready to help them. This new lady was going too far. So the whole city took up weapons against Matilda. She, with too much boldness and confidence, was just about to eat a well-cooked feast. But on hearing the noises from the city, she and all her followers ran away.

From Gesta Stephani.

Question Time

1. What happened to the country when Matilda and Stephen were fighting?

2. How did some of the barons take advantage of the troubles?

3. What do you learn from Source 2 about how women were supposed to behave in medieval times?

4. Source 3 describes Matilda and another woman. Who is the other woman?
   What do you learn from Source 3 about how women were supposed to behave in medieval times?

5. Why do you think that some barons did not keep their promise to support Matilda as successor to her father?

WHAT CHALLENGES DID MEDIEVAL MONARCHS FACE?

WHAT QUALITIES DID THEY NEED TO BE SUCCESSFUL?

In this Unit, you have found out the challenges faced by medieval monarchs in controlling the people and how successful they were. You have learnt about different methods of control that monarchs could use and some of the dangers they faced if they lost control.

Activity Time

❶ Royal children had tutors to teach them their lessons and to advise them about how they should behave. What advice might a tutor give to the royal children in his care?

- Write a list of challenges a royal child might face if he or she became monarch.
- Give advice about the qualities they must show to survive and succeed. This could include suggestions of what to do, and what not to do, if they have problems.

❷ Before you begin, write a profile of the pupil and their situation. Is the pupil: male or female; oldest, middle, youngest? What is the state of the country? Is it at peace or at war? Is it rich or poor? How large is the empire? Does the royal family have control of the borders?

Below is a list of some of the challenges monarchs might face.

- Some of the English barons do not want them.
- A Welsh prince leads a rebellion.

- Scots keep raiding the borders and damaging the land.
- Barons want the right to agree to taxation.
- No children to succeed to the throne.
- The Danish threaten to attack.
- The Pope and archbishops behave as if they are more powerful.
- Lack of money to fight wars.

❸ What other challenges might the pupil face? For example, a female pupil might face prejudice against her as queen.

In the advice you could include good ideas, skills and qualities. For example, think about what you could say about marriage, alliances with other countries, taxation, information, use of rewards. Look back through your work to find other ideas. Make sure your work is historically accurate. You should suggest medieval solutions to medieval problems. To do this you will need to use what you know about medieval people, what they thought and what they did.

Unit 3: How hard was life for medieval people in town and country?

In this Unit you are going to find out about how life was for most people in medieval times. For most, it was grim! Many people were like slaves and could not leave the land of their lord. Disaster was just around the corner. A bad harvest or flooding could mean starvation for thousands. Violence was also a great threat to a peaceful life. The poor were at the mercy of the rich and could be moved around or have their lands destroyed. Some of the most dramatic and shocking stories of British history are in this Unit, such as the plague that swept England like fire. And why, in the end, it might have been a good thing! There are other surprises – like a group of peasants murdering rich and important men and making demands of a king! For once, it seems, the boot was on the other foot.

WHAT DID MEDIEVAL ENGLAND LOOK LIKE?

Most villages were made up of peasants' houses, a church, a manor house and a mill. Only the manor house and church would be made of stone. The peasants' houses had mud and clay walls. The roofs were thatched. The roof and walls were supported by cruck beams. Each house had one or two rooms with a fire in the middle of one room. There were no chimneys and it must have been very smoky. Sometimes animals lived in the house, too. Each house would have a garden for growing small amounts of food.

Around each village were fields and small areas of wasteland. In the fields, crops such as corn and wheat were grown for food. As well as pigs, most peasants kept a few sheep and goats on the wasteland. The wasteland was land not ploughed for crop growing and each peasant had a share in it.

Although most medieval people lived in villages, a few lived in towns. There were far fewer towns in the Middle Ages than there are today. Towns were places of trade – places to buy and sell goods. Many had walls around them to protect trade, but in many ways towns were like large villages. Animals would have been common and most townspeople would also do some farming.

An artist's reconstruction of a peasant house.

WHAT DOES THE DOMESDAY BOOK TELL US ABOUT LIFE IN TOWN AND COUNTRY?

The Domesday Book is one of the most important documents for finding out about medieval life. It was written in 1086 on the instructions of William the Conqueror. He wanted information about land, people and animals in England. This is because he wanted to know how much tax he could get out of his kingdom.

William's officials travelled around the country asking questions about all the land, animals and people. They questioned the reeve, a man who looked after the lord's land. They also questioned the priest and six peasants. A second group then checked the answers. The officials were very careful to check the information in case it was wrong. Think about why a lord, knight or peasant might want to lie about the amount of land and number of animals they had. From the extract in Source 1, can you work out what a 'virgate' is?

- A wooden fence?
- A measurement of land?
- A religious man?

SOURCE 1

So very thoroughly did he have the inquiry carried out that there was not a single 'hide', not one virgate of land, not even one ox, nor one cow, nor one pig which escaped notice in his survey.

From the *Anglo-Saxon Chronicle*, written in the eleventh century.

TIME TRAVELLERS NEED TO KNOW THE LINGO!

This is another way that historians are like travellers. Sometimes people spoke a different language in the past. Historians have to work out what these words mean. In the Middle Ages, they used some different words. The feudal system organised people into different levels. Each level had a different relationship to the land. Each level of person had a different label which the Domesday Book used. Here is what two of these labels mean.

Villeins These were peasants who were not free. They were tied to the land of their lord. Villeins had to work on the lord's land. They had to do services for the lord and make payments to him. In return they were granted land to farm for themselves. Villeins could not leave the manor without the lord's permission. They needed the lord's permission for their daughters and sons to get married.

Freemen These were peasants who were free. Freemen paid rent to the lord for their land. They had to do some services for the lord. This was called 'boon work' and had to be done at very busy times like hay-making and harvest.

Some peasants were poorer than the villeins. They were called bordars or cottars. About one in ten peasants were slaves. This meant they had no property at all and had to do whatever work the lord demanded.

Question Time

1. Which peasants were not free?

2. Which peasants were free?

3. Start a glossary of medieval words. Put in:
   reeve   villein   freeman
   bordars and cottars   slaves

4. Historians have used the Domesday Book to calculate how many of the population were villeins, freemen, bordars or slaves and how much land they held. These are the figures that some historians have calculated:

	Per cent of population	Per cent of land
Slaves	9	No land
Bordars/cottars	32	5
Villeins/freemen	56	65
King, barons, church	3	30

Draw a pie chart to show how the land was divided up among the people.

5. The percentage share of the land used by peasants is bigger than the share of the land used by the king and barons. Does this mean that the peasants were richer?

6. Peasants were not all the same! Find two reasons why we can say this.

LAND IN THE DOMESDAY BOOK

There were different words for land as well as for people in the Domesday Book. Here are three.

Manor Large farm or estate in the hands of a lord. Manors were divided into demesne land and land granted to peasants.

Demesne This was the land of the lord that he did not grant to peasants to farm, but kept for himself. The villeins and slaves would look after this land for the lord.

Hide Measurement of land (120 acres, or 50 hectares). Larger than a virgate (30 acres, or 125 hectares).

The Domesday Book recorded the number of ploughs as well as the amount of land in acres. This was because the number of ploughs was a better sign of how rich the land was. Food can be grown on ploughed land, but it cannot be grown on all land. On rough, hilly land, for example, it is very hard to plant seeds and grow crops.

Add the following words to your glossary:
demesne   hide   virgate   plough

Here are some extracts from the Domesday Book about the countryside.

SOURCE 2

In Wallington, Fulco holds of Gilbert three hides and 40 acres of land. There is land for five ploughs. In demesne there are two ploughs, and four villeins with three ploughs. The three bordars have two ploughs. There is one cottar and two slaves. Altogether it is worth 50 shillings.

SOURCE 3

In 1086 there was wood for ten swine.

SOURCE 4

The mill at Stokesay gives nine loads of corn, and there is a miller.

SOURCE 5

At Alveston there is a fishery giving 1300 eels.

SOURCE 6

The manor of Ilford paid 16,000 herrings to the lord William of Warenne every year.

Other references in the Domesday Book mention beekeepers, hurdle-makers, and there is even one mention of a vineyard for growing grapes for wine!

Question Time

1 Why was William very interested in how rich the land was?

2 According to the Domesday Book, what different types of food could be eaten in medieval England?

3 Read Source 2 again. Use your glossary of medieval words to help you.
a Who are the poorest people in Wallington?
b Who is the richest person in Wallington?
c How much land is there?
d How many ploughs are needed for the lord's land?

4 Read Source 7 and compare it to Sources 2–6. In what ways was a town different from a manor? In what ways was a town similar to a manor?

5 Read Source 7. Free peasants, knights and lords could move freely around the country. Why would they want to visit a town?

6 Read Sources 2–6. Why did villeins, bordars, cottars and slaves not need to visit a town?

7 Imagine that it is 1087. William the Conqueror has died and William Rufus is king. He has just arrived in London and wants to know about his kingdom. He is very interested in how wealthy England is! This is because he wants to tax people to make money for himself. Write him a report explaining how the Domesday Book can help him.

SOURCE 7

Bury town is contained in a great circle of stone, including land which is ploughed and sown. Altogether there are 30 priests, 28 nuns who daily say prayers. 75 millers, ale-brewers, tailors, washerwomen, shoemakers, robe-makers, cooks, carriers, dispensers. Also there are 13 reeves over the land and under them 22 bordars.

WAS LIFE ALWAYS HARD FOR MEDIEVAL PEASANTS? HOW CAN WE FIND OUT?

The Domesday Book gives us very important information about medieval life, but it does not tell us everything. Think of three questions about the lives of medieval peasants that cannot be answered from the Domesday Book.

In order to find answers to these questions, we need to use other sources of information.

MEDIEVAL AND MODERN FARMERS

The fields around medieval villages did not look like most fields today. This is because they were farmed in a different way.

SOURCE 1

Two aerial photographs, one showing the medieval farming method of strip farming and the other showing the enclosed fields of modern day farming.

In most places in medieval times, fields were 'open' without hedges or fences. There were three 'open' fields around each village and each field was divided into strips. Each peasant farmed a few strips of each field. This was because each of the fields was different. One field was always fallow. Fallow meant left alone for the soil to rest. The soil needed to rest because the crops that grew on it took out the nutrients (goodness). Today most farmers use fertilisers to put back nutrients and the land does not need to rest. The other two fields would be ploughed and sown with crops such as wheat, rye and barley. Ploughing was done with oxen. Most peasants did not own the four or more oxen needed to make a team. They would get together with other peasants in the village to make up a team.

SOURCE 2

English peasants had punctured holes decorating their skin, short hair, shaved beards, golden bracelets. They drank too much ale.

This account is from William of Malmesbury, in the eleventh century.

SOURCE 3

Almost everything peasants needed had to be made at home, or by one of the villagers. Every village had its blacksmith, carpenter and others with special jobs. The only essential goods brought in from outside were salt and iron. Otherwise each village was self-supporting. Most peasants travelled more than a few miles, to the nearest market town.

This is a description of a medieval village by a modern historian in 1972.

SOURCE 4

This picture from the Luttrell Psalter shows peasants reaping and binding corn into sheaves.

SOURCE 5

*I have no pennies to buy pullets,
Nor geese nor pigs, but I have two green cheeses,
A few curds of cream, a cake of oatmeal,
Two loaves of beans and bran, baked for my children,
But I have parsley and pot herbs and plenty of cabbages,
And a cow and a calf.
This is the little we must live on till the Lammas season.
Poor folk in hovels,
Charged with children and overcharged by landlords,
What they may save by spinning they spend on rent,
On milk, or on meal to make porridge.*

This is an extract from the poem 'Piers Plowman' by William Langland, written in the fourteenth century.

SOURCE 6

In the manor of Borley, Essex, peasants perform these services for the lord: three days' work each week ploughing, carrying manure, weeding corn, mowing the meadow, reaping.

From Manor Court records of the fourteenth century.

Question Time

1. Although there were fewer people in medieval England than there are today, there was also less food to go around. Why?

2. Using all the information in the Unit so far, answer this question: In what ways was life hard for medieval peasants?

3. Make up your own true/false statements about 'Life for medieval peasants'. Try them out on your classmates to see how well you have understood the work. Then turn all your false statements into true ones.

Activity Time

1. Look at the picture in Source 7 of the village of Boarstall. Make a sketch of the village. Label the following on your sketch: church, peasant houses, mill, fields (with strips), woodland, demesne, manor.

2. Put boxes around your plan of a medieval village and fill in brief and important information about the village. For example, draw an arrow from a box to the mill. Inside you could write 'The mill was used to grind corn to make flour for bread.' Make sure the boxes are big enough for what you want to write, or do the writing first and then draw the box.

3. Read the paragraph that follows about medieval life. Each sentence uses one of the following sources of information: Domesday Book, archaeology, poetry, Manor Court records. Match each sentence to the source of information the historian has used.

In the village of Gelly there was enough land for six ploughs. The peasants who are villeins had to do three days' work each week ploughing, weeding and harvesting. They were so poor that they could hardly feed their children. Only two buildings in the village were made of stone.

SOURCE 7

A medieval picture of Boarstall, a small medieval village.

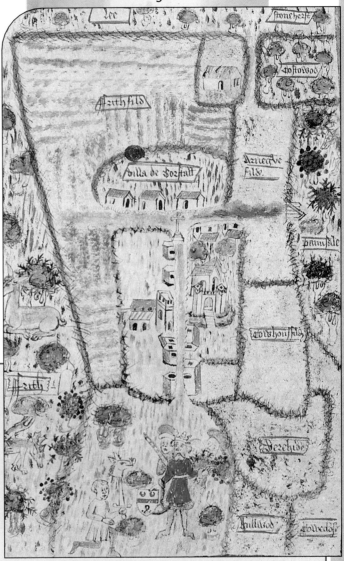

WAS LIFE ANY BETTER IN A MEDIEVAL TOWN?

Although most people lived in the countryside, the Middle Ages was a very important time for towns. Towns got bigger and there were more of them. Towns changed. They were not the same in the fifteenth century as they had been in the eleventh.

On page 64, you found out about Bury town by using the Domesday Book. You found out that some towns had fields inside the walls and most of the people grew food and had animals. In London, the law court stopped working at harvest time so that Londoners could bring in the corn from the fields!

HOW WERE TOWNS DIFFERENT FROM VILLAGES?

An artist's reconstruction of Salisbury in the Middle Ages.

Towns were places for buying and selling. Towns had markets where goods were exchanged for money or for other goods. Peasants would come to the market and exchange food for shoes, salt, cloth and iron pans. Buying and selling went on in shops as well as markets. Craftspeople, such as shoemakers, usually had a shop with rooms to live in above. The workroom, where the goods were made, was on the ground floor. In some towns all the shops on the street were of the same kind. For example, the shoemakers would be on one street, all the tailors on another street.

PROTECTING TRADE

Towns were usually well defended. This is because tradesmen needed to protect their goods and money. Towns had walls around with gates in. Strangers entering the town were asked questions about what they were doing there. At the same time, towns wanted people to visit and buy goods!

Some of the 'outsiders' were foreign tradesmen. They brought goods from the continent to sell in large cities and ports like London and Newcastle. It was so dangerous to travel by sea at this time that many of the foreign tradesmen formed groups to help and protect each other. The Hanseatic League was one of these groups. They brought fish, timber, furs and other goods from northern Europe.

Sometimes the people in a town would become very angry with groups of 'outsiders'. They would blame them for all the things that went wrong in the town. Sometimes they rioted against the 'outsiders'. For example, there were riots against Italians, French and Flemings in London during the Middle Ages.

In the twelfth century there were terrible riots against Jews living in English cities. In York many Jews were murdered and some committed suicide during riots. Some Christians did not like Jews. They had a different religion and culture. They did things differently. Some Jews had become rich by lending money to people, like banks do today. This made some people angry and jealous.

FROM VILLEIN TO FREEMAN

A villein could run away to a town. If he could support himself for one year and a day and pay his taxes, he became free. His lord could not force him back to the manor when he was free.

Towns were full of rules. Some of these rules were to protect the town and keep it safe. Others were to make life safe and fair for everyone in the towns. Those who broke the rules were punished by the town court. For example, bakers who cheated their customers could be put in the pillory with dough tied around their necks.

Question Time

Using the information on pages 68 and 69, write down five differences between towns and villages.

DIRTY, DARK AND DANGEROUS?

The streets of towns were very dirty. People emptied all their waste (including toilet waste) into the street. Nobody cleaned the streets, which were very narrow dirt paths. Often the dirt got into the river, which was also used for drinking. The houses of the town poor were made of mud and clay with thatched roofs. They usually had one room where everyone lived together. The houses of the rich were often made of stone and might have gardens and orchards. Sometimes their houses had tiled floors and glass windows.

All towns had taverns (pubs) which stayed open until dark. When it got dark, most people went home because the streets were dangerous. Towns had churches, and lots of them! Norwich had 50 churches. The churches were made of stone and were often the tallest and grandest buildings in the town.

Most towns had a fair once a year. This was a chance to be entertained as well as buy and sell goods. Many peasants would come to the fair to watch jugglers, wrestling matches, dancing bears and puppet shows.

WHAT WERE TOWN GUILDS?

Most towns had guilds. These were groups of craftsmen with their own rules. Different groups of craftsmen set up their own guilds, for example, there were guilds of carpenters, haberdashers (buyers and sellers of clothing or sewing accessories) and weavers. The rules were made to encourage and protect their craft.

Guilds organised entertainment as well as protecting their craft. They had special days when they would dress up and eat huge feasts! They also performed plays. These used stories from the Bible and were called 'miracle' plays. The plays would be made up of different stories and take several days to perform.

Activity Time

Answering important historical questions

Below is a list of important questions about medieval towns. In order to answer historical questions, we have to pick out bits of information that are relevant. 'Relevant' means bits of information that really answer the question!

Choose one of the questions below to research.
• How clean and healthy were medieval towns?
• How did town people spend their leisure time?
• How were outsiders treated by people in medieval towns?
• What rules did medieval towns have and why?
• How did people make money in medieval towns?
• What were buildings like in medieval towns?
• How safe were medieval towns?

Start answering your question by picking out the relevant information from this Unit. You could extend your research by using other sources of information. What else would you like to know about your topic? How could you find out?

You need to think carefully about how you will organise and present your findings.

• Collect the information.
• Organise it into: order of importance; or chronological order (order of dates); or a mixture of both.
• Consider how you will present your findings: with words, pictures, diagrams, charts or graphs?

WHY DID TOWNS GROW IN THE MIDDLE AGES?

During the Middle Ages, the number of towns in Britain doubled. Many of the towns that existed in the eleventh century were much bigger by the fourteenth century.

The main reason towns grew was because there was more trade. Manors were making more food than they needed, and the extra food was sold at market. This meant more buying and selling. More buying and selling meant some people had more money. They spent the money on buildings.

There were other reasons why towns grew. Castle-building led to new towns. Castles were good for trade. Builders, carpenters and other craftspeople were needed, as well as markets for food. Many towns in Wales grew because of the castles built by Edward I.

The growth of the wool and cloth industry in the Middle Ages also made towns grow. Many towns were built near rivers where mills could be built for making cloth. Towns were also places where wool and cloth were bought and sold.

Question Time

Copy the diagram and fill in the blanks to show the reasons why towns grew.

Why did towns grow?

Manors made extra food. →	Extra food sold at market. →	People had more money to spend. →	Towns grew because there were more shops and markets.
Castle-building →	→	→	Towns grew because...
Growth of cloth and wool trade →	→	→	Towns grew because...

Activity Time

Now you are going to compare life in a medieval village with life in a town. Get into pairs. One of you is a town dweller. You have a market stall selling cloth. You are poor, but hope to make more and more money as the town grows. One of you is a villein who lives in a village. You do not like being obedient to your lord. You are thinking of running away to the town.

Each of you must then
- Make a list of things you like about where you live.
- Make a list of things you do not like about where you live.

Have a conversation about whether the villein should move to the town or not.

1 Write a paragraph describing your conversation.

2 What were the main points in favour of town life?

3 What were the main points in favour of village life?

WHY WAS THE BLACK DEATH SO TERRIFYING?

Who or what is shown in the picture?
What are they doing? What did it mean?

An image of death as the grim reaper, from a sixteenth-century stained glass window.

THE HISTORY OF DEATH

In our society, science has helped us to understand the causes of death. A greater understanding of how the body works means that we can find out the causes of many illnesses and deaths. We know that germs can be passed from one person to another and spread disease. Although we cannot cure all diseases, we can treat many diseases with medicine. We also understand that each person has an immune system which fights illness. We know that people can become immune to diseases that they have been in contact with. We also know how to inoculate for some diseases to make people immune.

This was not the case in the Middle Ages. People did not have the scientific knowledge and understanding that we have today. As you have found out, people at that time looked at the world very differently. The Church taught people how to think about everything, including death.

Illness and death were unpredictable. Nobody could tell when they might come or how to prevent them. And if that wasn't bad enough, they blamed themselves, too! In their eyes, illness, death and famine were caused by God. So, illness, famine or death could mean that God was very angry with you.

THE BLACK DEATH OF 1349

In the year 1348 deaths from plague were recorded in the town of Melcombe Regis, Dorset. In the following year, the plague spread through England, Wales and Scotland as quickly as fire. It became known as the Black Death of 1349.

SOURCE 2

Bodies being buried at Tournai during the Black Death.

Those who caught it died within three or four days. Their symptoms could include swellings as big as apples in their armpits and groin and blue-black patches on their skin. Some of the people who caught the plague vomited blood. To try to protect themselves from catching it, people prayed to God or made pilgrimages.

Some people tried medicines, like herbs or vinegar, or even the innards of dead animals, to protect themselves against the plague. But these treatments did not work because people did not understand how the plague spread.

FLEAS, RATS AND SHIPS

The plague was carried on fleas that lived on black rats. Black rats came into England on ships. Ships from countries that had the plague, such as Italy, landed in English ports like Melcombe Regis. Once the plague had infected a few people in England, it was impossible to stop it.

So many people died that the graveyards of large towns like London quickly filled up. Big trenches had to be dug for the victims of the plague. The trench diggers were paid a lot of money to do their work! In the countryside, dead bodies could be seen in the fields and by the side of the road.

The Black Death of 1349 was followed by other outbreaks of plague in 1361, 1368 and 1375. The 1361 plague was called 'The Pestilence of Children' because more children died than adults. Plague kept on breaking out up until the Great Fire of London in 1666.

Question Time

1 Read the two answers below. They are both answering the same question: Why did people in medieval England let plague into the country?

People in medieval England must have been stupid. All they had to do to stop the plague was keep ships from landing in England.

People in medieval England thought differently from us. That is why they did not stop ships from landing in England.

Which is the better answer? Try to give one or two reasons for your choice.

2 Read the paragraph on the history of death again. Why were children more likely to die than adults in the second outbreak of plague?

HOW MANY PEOPLE DIED?

We do not know exactly how many people died. In the Middle Ages there were no records kept of population figures. However, historians can try to work out how many people died from using different sorts of evidence. For example, archaeology shows that many villages were abandoned at this time or shortly after. Over 100 abandoned villages have been discovered so far in Lincolnshire. The Church did keep records of the number of clergy (priests, rectors, vicars) who died. In Lincolnshire, 40 per cent of the clergy died.

SOURCE 4

The population of this island does not appear to bear any proportion to her fertility and riches.

A comment made by a visitor to England from Venice in 1500.

SOURCE 3

An aerial photo of Middle Ditchford, Gloucestershire, a village deserted during the Black Death. Outlines of buildings and fields are visible.

Historians think that the population fell by about one-third from 3.5 million before 1349 to about 2.5 million by 1500.

Question Time

How could historians use:
a archaeology
b church records
to try and work out how many people died in the plague?

WHAT DID PEOPLE THINK CAUSED THE PLAGUE?

People in the Middle Ages did not know about germs or how germs spread diseases. So, they had other explanations for the causes of the plague.

Many people thought that the plague was sent by God as a punishment for sins. The Bible has many stories of God punishing people, sometimes with plague. Some people whipped themselves to try to stop plague spreading. Some people thought that the Jews had caused the plague. They said that the Jews had poisoned the water. In some parts of Europe, Jewish people were murdered to try to stop the plague spreading. In London the human waste that was lying around in the streets was cleaned away. This was done by people who thought the plague was caused by dirty air.

All of the explanations they thought of at the time were wrong! None of them caused the plague. However, these ideas are still very useful to us. We can use them to find out about medieval people. We can use them to find out what and how medieval people thought.

Question Time

Look at the boxes below. On the left are reasons that medieval people gave as causes for the plague. On the right are descriptions of how medieval people thought.

Reasons for plague	What/how medieval people thought	What they did to solve the problem
God is angry	Some medieval people thought that God controlled everything. If he sent plague it was a punishment for wrong-doing. If he sent a good harvest it was because the people had been good.	
Dirty/bad air	Some medieval people thought that illness and good health depended on the four elements of air, earth, water, fire. The plague spread through dirty air.	
Jewish people	Some medieval people persecuted minority groups and blamed them when life was difficult. Jewish people were a minority in Europe and they got blamed for the plague.	

❶ Fill in the third column by describing what they did to solve the problem.

❷ Which solution might have helped?

❸ In Florence, Italy, sick people were banned from coming into the city. But the plague still spread. Why do you think this happened?

Activity Time

Why was the Black Death so frightening? Your turn to decide!

Below are statements about the Black Death. Read all the statements. As you read, think about whether the statement is a cause of the Black Death, a description of the Black Death (symptoms, how people reacted and so on), or a result of the Black Death.

❶ Write out all the statements in the box and label them cause, description or result.

> *People prayed and went on pilgrimages to stop themselves catching the plague.*
>
> *The plague came into England on ships from the continent.*
>
> *Most people died very quickly, within three or four days.*
>
> *Symptoms of plague were big lumps under armpits and in the groin, black and blue blotches, vomiting blood.*
>
> *The plague was carried by fleas on the black rat.*
>
> *In the fourteenth century, people did not know how to stop the plague from spreading.*
>
> *The plague was worse in the towns where people lived closer to each other.*
>
> *The number of people in Britain (population) decreased because of the plague. Probably about one-third of the people died.*
>
> *The plague came back in 1356, 1361, 1368 and 1375. It carried on coming back until the Great Fire of London in 1666.*
>
> *The 1361 plague was called the 'Pestilence of Children' because children were more likely to die from it than adults.*
>
> *Some people blamed the Jews for the plague.*
>
> *Some people thought God had sent the plague.*
>
> *Some people whipped themselves to try to stop the plague spreading.*
>
> *Some cities banned visitors from coming in, but the plague still spread.*
>
> *Whole villages were abandoned because of the plague.*
>
> *The Black Death was a very important turning point in the history of the Middle Ages. This is because it changed life very dramatically.*

❷ Now write out three paragraphs that answer the question: Why was the Black Death so frightening? Organise your paragraphs into causes, description and results.

WAS THE BLACK DEATH A GOOD THING FOR THOSE WHO SURVIVED?

Historians today call the Black Death a 'turning point' in our history. This means that it led to lots of changes. England was different after the Black Death. Instead of saying that the Black Death made life even grimmer, they say it made life less grim for those who survived. Although over a million people died, the Black Death was also a good thing. The people who survived had a better standard of living because of the plague. As a result of the number of plague deaths there were fewer people in England, which meant more food and land for those who were left.

BEFORE 1349
3.5 million people

AFTER 1349
2.5 million people

Look at the pictures of the two loaves of bread. They explain why people after 1349 would have had more bread to eat. Remember that England was getting crowded by 1300! In 1315 there had been a very bad famine, so more bread was needed to feed everyone and peasants were needed to plant the corn, reap it, grind it into flour and bake it into bread. All the peasants who took part in making the bread needed to be paid. This was another reason that life got better after 1349. Wages – the amount people got paid for their work – also increased. So not only was there more food to go around – but food was cheaper, too!

I need workers to farm my land.

There are a lot of us workers around. I'm lucky to get work. I'll work for 2 pence a day.

There aren't enough of us workers around. That lord will be lucky to have me. I want to be paid 5 pence a day.

Question Time

1 Look at the cartoon picture on page 78.

   a Is the large group showing peasants before or after 1349?

   b Is the small group showing peasants before or after 1349?

   c Which group will be paid the higher wages?

   d Why?

2 Here is a sequence of statements that explain how the Black Death made life better. The first and last statements are in order but the others need to be put in the correct order. Write them out in an order that answers the question.

3 The Black Death made life harder for many lords. Why do you think this happened?

'How did the Black Death make life better for peasants?'

1 The Black Death killed about one-third of the population of England.

Fewer people meant there were fewer peasants to work the land.

This meant there were fewer people buying food.

So, the lords had to pay more to get workers.

Fewer people buying food meant food was cheaper.

Peasants had more money to spend because wages were higher and food was cheaper.

7 The Black Death made life better for peasants because they became richer and more powerful.

WHY WAS THERE A PEASANTS' REVOLT IN 1381?

Look carefully at Source 1 on page 80. It shows events in 1381.

The man in the centre of the picture wearing a crown is King Richard II. He was fourteen years old. The man on his left wearing a grey hat is Wat Tyler. Wat Tyler was the leader of the Peasants' Revolt. What is about to happen to Wat Tyler? Is there anything strange about the picture? Who do you think are the crowd of people on the right?

The picture shows two events! It is like a cartoon without a line down the middle. The left side happened first. It shows Richard II meeting Wat Tyler at Smithfield in London. Wat Tyler asked the king for some changes. Wat Tyler was then murdered by the Mayor of London. The right side happened next. Richard rode up to the crowd and spoke to them. The crowd were all peasants, but the drawing shows them in armour, like an army. This was not how they really looked. We know from other sources that most of them did not have armour, but wore smocks and jerkins. Richard II is not drawn accurately either. Look carefully at his face. How is his face different in the two sides of the picture? Why do you think he looks different?

SOURCE 1

A painting showing the events at Smithfield when Richard II met Wat Tyler in 1381.

A SURPRISING STORY

Think about what you know about medieval kings and their relationship to the peasants. Make a list of all the things that are surprising about the story so far.

Just before the king met Tyler, there had been some other murders. The Archbishop of Canterbury and other royal ministers, including the king's chancellor, were beheaded in the Tower. Their heads were put on stakes mounted on London Bridge where they could be easily seen.

Just before the archbishop was murdered, thousands of peasants had marched on London. They burned the houses of rich people and murdered many of them.

The Peasants' Revolt is a very surprising story. This is because it challenged medieval ideas about how people should be. In medieval times, people were supposed to know their place! Not only were they supposed to know their place, they were also supposed to stay there! Very few peasants ever became knights and very few knights ever became barons. But the peasants were not happy with the way things were.

WHY WERE THE PEASANTS SO UNHAPPY?

There are many different reasons why the Peasants' Revolt happened and challenged medieval ideas so dramatically. Your task is to sort out the reasons and use them to explain why the Revolt happened.

Historians organise reasons into different groups to help them understand what happened. There are long-term causes. These are things that have been going on for a long time. There are short-term causes. These are things that happen just before the big event.

Read the information below. Which do you think were long-term causes of the Peasants' Revolt?

Which do you think were short-term causes of the Peasants' Revolt?

• Young king and bad advisers
Richard II was only ten years old when he became king in 1377. Because he was so young, he relied on advisers. These advisers gave very bad advice about how to treat the people!

• Losing war
When Richard became king, England had been at war with France for nearly 50 years. The war started to go very badly for England after 1369.

• Expensive war
The war had cost a lot and it was still costing a lot of money.

• New religious ideas
Some priests in the Church were criticising medieval beliefs. One priest, John Ball, went around saying that all men were equal to each other! There was a lot of enthusiasm for his ideas.

• Black Death
The Black Death of 1349 had made many peasants richer and more powerful. They wanted higher wages to work on the lord's land.

• Unfree peasants
Many peasants had been able to buy their freedom from the lord after 1349. Not all peasants had been able to do this and were still unfree. Now they wanted to be free too.

• Keeping wages down
The lords did not want to pay higher wages. In 1351 a law was passed limiting the maximum wage. Peasants could not ask for more than this as pay for their work.

• Poll Taxes of 1377 and 1379
In 1377 and 1379 Poll Taxes were introduced. This was a tax on every person. It did not matter how rich or poor they were. Everyone had to pay 4d. This was a lot of money for most peasants to pay.

- Poll Tax of 1381

In 1381 a third Poll Tax was introduced! Some peasants in Essex attacked a Poll Tax collector. A judge and some lords were murdered. In Kent similar violence happened. Then thousands of peasants marched on London.

1369   1377   1379

Bomb
LONG-TERM CAUSES

Activity Time

1 Copy out the drawing above. Below the bomb write a list of the long-term causes. These are things that had been going on for a long time before 1381. They are causes but they might not have led to revolt on their own.

2 Write out headings of the causes. Do not use full sentences. For example, instead of writing: 'The war had cost a lot and was still costing a lot of money,' write 'expensive war'.

3 Along the fuse write the short-term causes. These are things that happened very close to 1381 and made the peasants angry.

4 But the fuse still needs a match to light it! Write near the match the event that made the peasants' anger explode in 1381.

WAS THE REVOLT SUCCESSFUL?

Look back to the picture of Richard II talking to the peasants. Apparently the conversation went something like this:

Wat Tyler: 'We have two demands: All villeins must be made free and rent for land must be fixed at 2d an acre.'

Richard II: 'You may have your demands. I agree!'

Then Wat Tyler was killed. Richard rode over to the peasants.

Richard II: 'You may have your demands. I promise you! Now go home.'

The peasants did go home. But Richard II broke his promise. Soldiers were sent out to arrest any peasants still in London. Then the king and his soldiers rode into the countryside. They rounded up the leaders of the revolt and hanged them. Their bodies were left on gibbets to rot as a warning to others.

WHAT HAPPENED TO JOHN BALL?

The priest John Ball was captured and put on trial. He admitted taking part in the revolt, and on 15 July 1381 he was put to death by hanging.

THE PEASANTS WHO REVOLTED: ARE THEY STILL HEROES?

Although many medieval people were shocked at the Peasants' Revolt, the peasants have become heroes for some people today, especially for people who are angry about things in our society and want to change it.

The Poll Tax can still spark off riots and rebellions today! When Mrs Thatcher introduced the Poll Tax in Scotland in 1989 and in England and Wales in 1990, 15 million people did not pay it. One quarter of a million people came to demonstrate against the Poll Tax in London, and this led to one of the biggest riots in our history. Six months later Mrs Thatcher lost power. The Poll Tax was one of the reasons!

Question Time

Many surviving accounts of the revolt were written from the side of the king, not the peasants.

❶ Write an account of the Peasants' Revolt that is from the peasants' side.

Think about:
- How will you describe the king and what he did?
- How will you describe Tyler and what happened to him?
- What will you say about the causes of the revolt?

❷ Think about what sort of a person John Ball was. He was quoted as saying: 'John Miller, John Carter, John Nameless – all equal with other men.' What do you think he meant by this?

❸ Why was the Poll Tax seen as unfair by people in both 14th- and 20th-century Britain?

HOW HARD WAS LIFE FOR MEDIEVAL PEOPLE IN TOWN AND COUNTRY?

Many films and television stories have been made that are set in medieval Britain. For example, *First Knight*, *Robin Hood*, *Ivanhoe* and the *Brother Cadfael Mysteries*.

These films can be very useful for helping us picture what medieval Britain looked like, because it was so different from today. At the same time, many films which are set in medieval times are not historically accurate. This means they do not show medieval Britain as it really was.

Look at the picture on page 84. In what ways is it not an accurate picture of medieval life? Why do you think film makers might not want to show medieval life accurately?

A still from the 1995 film, *First Knight*.

Activity Time

You are the researcher for a Hollywood film company. It wants to make a film set in the Middle Ages. Your job is to research historical background for the film.

You receive the following instructions from the director:

Dear Researcher

How are things in jolly little England? We do envy you your history. All those quaint old villages. Just the right setting for our next film. Now apparently I missed getting that Oscar last year because I was careless over historical detail. Hah! I don't want that happening again, so I'm relying on you to help me out. Between you and me, I'm very confused. I've looked at a few pictures and either the peasants are having a jolly good time dancing around maypoles and getting drunk or they're dressed in rags and being pushed around like slaves. Now tell me – which version do I believe? HELP!

Don't let me down now. I need:

Scene 1
Set in a medieval village.
What would the peasants be doing?
What would their houses look like?
What other buildings would be there?
What clothes would they be wearing?
What would the landscape around be like?
What would be going on in the fields?

Scene 2
Set in a medieval town.
What would the people be doing?
What would their houses look like?
What other buildings would be there?
What clothes would they be wearing?

For both the scenes I need advice about sound effects. By the way, I don't mind which part of England the film is set in – you decide!

Looking forward to hearing from you.

Susannah Vincente

Use all the information in this Unit to give background information for the two scenes. You will need to make some choices. For example: What time of year is it in the village? Is it time for ploughing/sowing/harvesting?

In the town, is it a fair day or a market day or neither?

You might want to provide plans/drawings/maps to help explain your ideas.

Write a letter to go with your background information. In the letter you should make sure you answer her question:

'I've looked at a few pictures and either the peasants are having a jolly good time dancing around maypoles and getting drunk or they're dressed in rags and being pushed around like slaves. Now tell me – which version do I believe?'

Unit 4: How did the medieval church affect people's lives?

WHY HAVE SO MANY MEDIEVAL CHURCHES SURVIVED UNTIL TODAY?

SOURCE 1

This is a modern aerial photograph of Durham Castle and Cathedral. What would it have looked like in medieval times without all the houses and streets around it? Make an image of the cathedral and castle as they might have looked 600 years ago. You could trace the medieval buildings and use them as a basis of a picture, or you could scan the photograph and remove all the modern buildings. then see if you can answer the questions below.

What was the cathedral built from?

What were the houses built from?

Why was the cathedral so large?

What does the castle tell you about power?

Why did the people in Durham build their cathedral to last for longer than their houses?

Why has the castle been built so close to the cathedral?

What does the cathedral tell you about power?

POWER SHARING IN DURHAM?

A castle and a cathedral sharing the same site – why did this happen here? It was all due to the Normans. They needed to control the Saxon kingdoms of England and one of the ways they did this was to build a series of motte and bailey castles. (Look back to pages 33–34 and remind yourself of this.) The rebellious and war-like north of England was particularly troublesome to them. Between 1069 and 1070, the Normans had carried out a fearsome policy of burning crops and homes, and killing animals and people. This was later called the 'Harrying of the North'. You read about this on pages 40 and 41. The Normans had to find sites for their castles that were as protected as possible, but which at the same time commanded the surrounding countryside. In Durham they found an ideal spot – a craggy, high piece of land surrounded on three sides by the River Wear – and in 1072 began building. The Normans needed to show that they, not the defeated Saxons, were the power in the land.

But the site the Normans had chosen had been chosen seventy-five years earlier by the Saxons, and for something entirely different. Monks took the body of St Cuthbert, who had once been Bishop of Lindisfarne, and buried it in the very first Durham Cathedral. The cathedral building you can see in the picture on page 87, which the Normans began building in 1093, was really the second cathedral. Master masons, stone masons, craftsmen and labourers worked away, year after year. Many died of old age and illness. Some were killed on the site by falling stone and collapsing wooden scaffolding. Others drifted off. But work on the building continued until, in 1137, the cathedral was finished.

THE LAND OF THE PRINCE-BISHOPS

Who was in control? The prince in the castle, or the bishop in the cathedral? The solution was simple: neither of them and both of them. There was only one person in control: the Prince-Bishop. He lived in the castle, and was both prince over the land and bishop in the cathedral. One day he could be killing Scottish marauders in the Borders (the disputed land between England and Scotland), and the next, taking Mass in the cathedral.

THE WICKED STORY OF WALCHER

Walcher was the first Prince-Bishop at Durham. He didn't have a very happy, or specially holy, life. People suspected him of being involved in the rather nasty murder of a Saxon. Eventually the man's family caught up with Walcher and demanded a face-to-face meeting.

Reluctantly, suspecting a trap, Walcher agreed to meet them in a church at Gateshead. As soon as Walcher was inside the church, the Saxons sprung the trap. Slamming the doors shut and pulling a great beam across them so that Walcher couldn't get out, they set fire to the piles of dry brushwood piled against the church walls. Gasping and choking, with his eyes red and stinging and his lungs full of stinking smoke, Walcher had to think quickly. Should he stay inside the church and risk burning to death or try to escape and risk death at the hands of the Saxons outside? He was, after all, a Prince-Bishop, and maybe the Saxons would look on him more as a bishop than as a murderer. He was wrong. The Saxons were waiting, knives and clubs at the ready. When Walcher, scorched and nearly blinded, staggered out through the dense, swirling black smoke, they fell on him. Kicking, stamping, stabbing and clubbing, they avenged their dead kinsman. Swearing, cursing and pleading, Walcher didn't take long to die.

WAS IT LIKE THIS EVERYWHERE?

No, it wasn't! There were holy, just and wise bishops and archbishops as well as wicked and cruel ones. Some were rich and powerful; others were poor and needy. In between came the churchmen who did their best and sometimes failed and sometimes succeeded, but generally just muddled through.

WHAT WAS CHRISTENDOM?

When you have worked through Question Time on page 92, you'll know that there were Christian churches of all shapes and sizes from Kirkwall in the Orkneys to Istanbul in what is now Turkey, and in medieval times was part of the Ottoman Empire. Most people living in Europe were Christians and belonged to the Catholic Church. There were Christians living in other parts of the world, but the part of the world where most Christians lived was Europe and the Church called this Christendom.

WAS EVERYONE A CHRISTIAN?

No, they weren't! Outside western Europe there were people who believed just as deeply in their own religions and faiths as the Christians did in theirs. For example, during the twelfth century, Muslim travellers carried their faith, Islam, from the Muslim heart-lands in the Middle East to southern Europe, north Africa and China. There were also Jews in every European country and they followed the ancient faith of Judaism.

This map shows you the extent of medieval Christendom. It is surrounded by pictures of medieval churches and cathedrals.

Northleach, Gloucestershire.

N

Church of the Madeleine

Santiago de Compostela

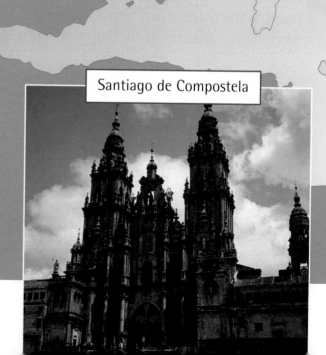

Hagia Sophia

KEY

Christendom

St Magnus, Kirkwall.

Jerusalem

- What is the same about these churches?
- What is different about these churches?
- Can you suggest reasons for the similarities and the differences?
- What do they tell you about Christendom?

Question Time

1. What conclusions can you draw about Christianity in medieval times from
   a the building and sites of Durham Cathedral and Castle
   b the Prince-Bishops of Durham?

2. Research Saxon punishments. How might one of the murdered Saxon's family have justified what he did to Walcher?

3. Copy the map on pages 90-91 and label the medieval churches into their right locations on the map. Show the area European Christendom covered in medieval times.

4. Go and look at your local parish church. When was it built? If it wasn't built before about 1500, find the medieval church nearest to where you live. Does it look anything like the pictures of medieval churches you put on the map of Europe? Can you start working out why it might have been built where it was?

WHAT IMPACT DID PARISH CHURCHES HAVE ON PEOPLE'S LIVES?

HOW IMPORTANT WAS THE PARISH CHURCH TO MEDIEVAL PEOPLE?

Look carefully at the picture and you can see how the church was one of the most important buildings in the village. What makes it so important? Is it because of its size? Is it because of where it is built in the village? Is it because of the materials from which it is built? Or are there any other reasons?

The church reminded people of their duty to God. Every day, whether people were working in the fields or at home, they heard the church bells ringing each hour. They saw its stone tower rising above their own wooden and wattle cottages and knew it would still be there when they and their cottages were long gone. Villagers went to the

SOURCE 1

A modern photo of Lyddington village showing the dominant position of the church.

parish church for all the important events in their lives. These are sometimes called rites of passage. Their parents took them to the church to be baptised by the priest when they were a few weeks old. In medieval times many babies died, and the belief was that babies who died before they were baptised could not go to heaven. Men and women were married in church and, in the church's holy ground, they would be buried when they died. It was to the church they went on holy days and on Sundays for Mass. It was in the church that people told the priest about the things they had done and thought that were wrong and he used his special powers to give them God's forgiveness for their sins.

WHAT IS MASS?

The Mass is central to Roman Catholic worship. It began in the days of the early Church, linked to Jesus Christ's last supper with His disciples, when He ate bread and wine with them. It was, and still is, the most important part of a Catholic church service. The priest blesses some bread and wine and offers them to God. At that moment, believers think that God miraculously changes the bread and wine into the blood and body of His son, Jesus Christ. This is called trans-substantiation. The priest eats some bread and drinks some wine on behalf of all the people in the church. He believes this unites them with Jesus Christ at that moment and brings them all into close communion with God.

WERE MEDIEVAL CHURCHES USED ONLY FOR RELIGIOUS SERVICES?

The church was really the centre of village life. People did not always get married inside the church. Sometimes couples married in the church porch so that the whole village could see them married and join in the fun afterwards in the churchyard. Sometimes people used their church building as a market place where they bought and sold goods and animals. They held feasts, fairs and drinking parties in the church and these often overflowed into the churchyard. Sometimes villagers used the church building as a theatre. They watched plays put on by travelling actors and joined in with the entertainments.

Question Time

1 Look back at the picture of the parish church (Source 1). Make a list, using only the picture, of the reasons why the church seems to be the most important building in the village. What does this tell us about the ways in which medieval people regarded the Christian religion?

2 Read about the different ways in which medieval people used their church buildings. For each activity, say where it would be held today. Why have all these activities moved out of the church building?

3 Research 'rites of passage' in the Christian religion and in the Jewish, Muslim and Hindu faiths. What are these rites? In what ways are they similar in all four faiths? Why are they important?

DID PARISH PRIESTS DO ANYTHING MORE THAN TAKE CHURCH SERVICES ON SUNDAYS AND HOLY DAYS?

It was a law of the Christian Church that priests lived by themselves without any family. This was because a priest was supposed to regard everyone in his parish as part of his family and therefore his responsibility. He had to look after their needs and so wouldn't have time for a wife and children of his own.

SOURCE 3

A stained glass window image of a priest treating the sick.

SOURCE 2

A medieval picture showing a parish priest conducting a burial.

SOURCE 4

He truly knew Christ's gospel and would
preach it
Devoutly to his parishioners.
He much disliked extorting tithe or fee,
Nay, rather he preferred beyond a doubt
Giving to poor parishioners round about
From his own goods and Easter offerings.
Wide was his parish, with houses far asunder,
Yet he neglected not in rain or thunder,
In sickness or in grief, to pay a call
On the remotest, whether great or small.
He did not run to London to earn easy bread
By singing masses for the wealthy dead.
Holy and virtuous he was, but then
Never contemptuous of sinful men,
Never disdainful, never too proud or fine.
His business was to show a fair behaviour
And draw men thus to heaven and their
Saviour.

In about 1386, Geoffrey Chaucer wrote a poem called 'The Canterbury Tales'. This is part of what he wrote about a parish priest.

NOT ALL PRIESTS WERE LIKE THE ONE GEOFFREY CHAUCER DESCRIBED!

SOURCE 5

The ignorance of the priests casteth the people into the ditch of error.

In 1281, Archbishop Peckham wrote this about parish priests.

SOURCE 6

He has been a parish priest for more than thirty years
But he cannot sing the Mass properly, nor read the Bible.
He can't explain the psalms to the people.
But he's good at hunting hares in the fields.

In about 1380, William Langland wrote about a parish priest in his poem 'Piers Ploughman'.

LATER WRITERS HAD DIFFERENT THINGS TO SAY ABOUT MEDIEVAL PARISHES AND THEIR PRIESTS.

SOURCE 7

In many parishes, the priest only stumbled through some homily or sermon four times a year. In a good many others, the evidence suggests neglect even of these most important four. With so feeble a guide, the villager could not get far on his quest for the Truth, and there is little wonder that villagers' religion was often a thing of use and wont – part sincere, part habit and part pure magic.

In 1937, H S Bennett wrote about parish priests in his book *Life on the English Manor.* This is part of what he said.

SOURCE 8

There were many priests who stayed in their parishes and were as good as Chaucer's parson. But this was not often the case. Life as a vicar was too hard to attract men of talent.

In 1973, Maurice Keen wrote about priets in his book *England in the Later Middle Ages.*

WERE PARISH PRIESTS PAID A SALARY BY THE CHURCH?

No, they weren't – not really. Obviously, priests needed money to survive, just as everybody else did, and they usually charged fees for baptisms, weddings and funerals. Priests then had to fill in the parish registers, saying who had been baptised, married or buried, and when. Sometimes they didn't fill in these registers until the end of the year, or over a wet weekend, and they got things a bit wrong! They kept the collection money at Easter and, when someone died, they could claim his second best animal.

Question Time

1. How reliable are Sources 2-7 as sources of evidence about the life of a medieval parish priest?

2. Would you agree with Maurice Keen that 'Life as a vicar was too hard to attract men of talent.'?

In a village parish, priests worked the land that belonged to the church. This was called the glebe land, and priests could grow crops and breed animals on it just as the other villagers did on their land. They argued about prices at the market and wanted to make as much profit as they could, just like everyone else. The priest had 'income' in other ways, too. Everyone had to give one-tenth of everything they produced to the Church. In the country, this was, for example, one-tenth of their grain and one-tenth of their wool. In the towns, it was one-tenth of the profit that craftsmen and traders made. The local priest collected the 'tithe'. Although most tithes went to the bishop to be used for the Church in general, about a quarter stayed in the parish and was used to help the local poor, sick and elderly. Some of the tithe helped to feed and clothe the parish priest, and keep a roof over his head.

Question Time

1 What different kinds of work did a medieval priest have to do? Make a spidergram, with the priest in the middle.

2 What personal qualities should a medieval priest have? Should he, for example, be cunning or straightforward, kind or strict, clever or simple? Make a second spidergram, linked in with the first one.

3 Use both these spidergrams to work out what advice a father might give to his son who has just told him he wants to become a parish priest. Write out what their conversation might be.

4 Why do you think that some priests fell below the standards expected of them?

SOURCE 9

The priest spends his time in taverns, and there his tongue is loosed to the great scandal of everyone. He is living with a woman, Margaret, and he cannot read or write and so cannot look after his parishioners' souls.

In 1397, the Bishop of Hereford listened to evidence from villagers living in the parishes under his control. This is what one villager said about his priest.

SOURCE 10

Ten of the villagers were each fined 2d because they made their sheaves of corn much smaller when they were putting them together for the tithe. They ought to have made them the same size as they did when working for the Lady of the Manor.

This source, from court records, tells us what villagers in Foxton, Cambridgeshire, did to cheat the Church out of tithes.

WHAT WERE CHURCHES LIKE INSIDE?

There were many different sorts of churches: some large and grand and some small and simple. Most Saxon churches had been made from wood and these were gradually replaced with stone ones. New churches built in medieval times were usually built from stone. All churches were built in the shape of a cross with the altar at the east end unless the site was difficult to build on.

Churches were built to glorify God and were usually large enough to take two or three times the number of people in the parish. People gathered in the main body of the church, the nave, to worship and to listen to the parish priest. There were no pews or chairs, and so men, women and children stood in small groups or knelt on the rush-strewn stone floor. The east end of the church, known as the chancel, where the priest celebrated the Mass, was especially holy. The people did not enter this area.

As England grew richer and some individual parishes grew very prosperous, side aisles to the nave were built, so that there could be religious processions around the church. They replaced the plain glass in the windows with stained glass and put beautifully embroidered cloths and gold candlesticks on the altar. People painted scenes from the Bible straight on to the plain stone walls, decorated the pillars and arches with bright patterns and made huge 'doom' paintings warning people of the horrors of hell and showing them the delights of heaven. All these things made the church very different from any other building in the parish.

Over the centuries, the Catholic Church became immensely strong and powerful. Eventually, it was the richest and largest landowner in Christendom, and collected its own taxes and made its own laws – canon law. But its real strength was in the power it had over people's minds.

SOURCE 11

Why should I want to go to heaven? I would not wish to go there unless I can have Nicolette, because I love her so much. I want nothing to do with the sort of people who will go to heaven, doddering old priests and fools who grovel in church all day and night. I'd rather be in Hell with those handsome knights killed in battle and other noblemen, with those lovely noble ladies who have lots of lovers.

This is part of a popular medieval story. A young man called Aucassin has been told that, if he keeps seeing his girlfriend, he most certainly won't go to heaven and might go to hell!

Question Time

1 Why were churches built bigger than they needed to be to hold all the people in a parish?

2 Research to find out why churches were built in the shape of a cross and why the altar was always at the east end of the church.

HOPES OF HEAVEN AND FEARS OF HELL: WHAT DID PEOPLE BELIEVE?

Very few people in medieval times could read. There was no need to. But this meant that people had to remember what they were told. Normally this wouldn't be a problem. 'Drive the sheep to Ridgeback Hill', 'Remember to milk the cows before sundown' or even 'The best leather in Lincoln is sold by Edgar from his stall by the cathedral's west door', wouldn't have been too difficult to remember. But what about complicated ideas? How could the Christian Church tell people who couldn't read, that heaven and hell were real places and that the only way to share in the joys and delights of heaven was to obey the teachings of the Roman Catholic Church? How could the Church warn them of the awful fate in store for them if they disobeyed? The Church found the answer by using large, bright, detailed and terrifying wall-paintings. The paintings would be seen by every man, woman and child each time they went into their church. This would be at least once every Sunday and at other times during the week when the church building was used as market and as a meeting place.

SOURCE 12

A medieval doom painting. Paintings like these reminded ordinary people about the joys of heaven and horrors of hell.

SOURCE 13

To our left was dreadful with burning flames while the opposite side was equally horrible with raging hail and bitter snow blowing and driving in all directions. Both sides were filled with men's souls which seemed to be hurled from one side to the other by the fury of the tempest. Some dark spirits came from the fiery depths and terrified me with their glowing eyes and foul flames coming from their mouths and nostrils. Then my guide took me along a road to the right and brought me out of darkness into clear light. I saw a broad and lovely meadow flooding with light. And as my guide led me through the crowds of happy citizens, I began to wonder whether this was the Kingdom of Heaven.

From *A History of the English Church and People* written around 730 AD by the Venerable Bede. It is part of a story told by a man from Northumbria who thought he had returned from the dead.

DUST TO DUST, ASHES TO ASHES?

Death was very close to medieval people. Parents had large families and they could expect to see some of their children die. They themselves would be old at forty and probably dead by fifty. Famines and wars, plagues and diseases killed thousands. Many medieval people must have wondered about the meaning of life. They saw the cycle of the seasons – the 'birth' of life in spring, followed by summer, then autumn and the cold 'death' of winter, to be followed again by spring. Would their own life and their own death follow a similar pattern? The Christian Church gave them the answer: after death there was eternal life in heaven, where people's souls would worship and praise God for ever. But eternal life had to be earned.

Eternal life was given only to those people who had followed the teachings of the Christian Church when they were alive on earth. But even then it wasn't that simple. People who had been wicked and never asked for forgiveness for their sins went straight to hell when they died. Hell was a dreadful place, full of pain and suffering, where devils tormented people's souls for ever. Most people, the Church taught, were not evil enough for their souls to go straight to hell, nor good enough for their souls to go straight to heaven. So, they went to purgatory. This was a pretty dreadful place, but not as bad as hell. Souls stayed there, maybe for hundreds of years, until all their sins were burned away and their pure souls could enter heaven.

'FAST-TRACK' THROUGH PURGATORY?

People could speed up the time their souls spent in purgatory. They could build up 'credit' while they were alive, or, when they were dead, loving friends and relatives could help them on their way to heaven. The Church expected people to confess their sins, do penance (the punishment given them by the priest who heard their confession) and receive forgiveness. Beyond this, people could light candles in holy places, buy pardons from travelling pardoners, and make pilgrimages to holy places. Rich people could have special chapels built and could give money to help found monasteries and nunneries.

Question Time

1 What is happening in Source 12, the doom painting? Why is it called a doom painting?

2 How might ordinary medieval people react, seeing this painting nearly every day of their lives?

3 Why did pictures like this 'doom painting' play such an important part in the life of the medieval church?

4 Use the extract from the Venerable Bede's sermon to make a doom painting of your own.

5 Explain how the medieval Church tried to control what people believed in and what they did.

WHAT IMPACT DID MONKS AND NUNS HAVE ON PEOPLE'S EVERYDAY LIFE?

Medieval churches tell us something about the ways in which medieval people worshipped and what they believed in. In the same way, medieval monasteries and nunneries tell us something about the ways in which medieval monks and nuns spent their time in the service of their God. One of the problems, however, is that most of these buildings in Britain are in ruins.

What clues do the buildings give you about what happened there in medieval times?

SOURCE 1

Modern photographs of the ruins of Rievaulx (left) and Tintern Abbeys (bottom), and a contemporary engraving of Citeaux Abbey.

What similarities can you find between the buildings?

Are the buildings decorated in any way?

What are the building materials?

What shapes are the windows and doorways?

What differences can you find between the buildings?

Question Time

1 Choose ONE of the buildings. Find out when it was built, where it was built, by whom, and why, it was built.

2 Compare what you have found out with what others in your class have found out about that building and the other buildings. Build up an information database to which you can add later. These can either be written notes in a folder, or you can use ICT. Add to your databases as you work through this section of the Unit.

WHERE DID THE IDEA COME FROM THAT PEOPLE SHOULD DEVOTE THEIR LIVES TO GOD BY LIVING IN SEPARATE COMMUNITIES?

Christians began getting away from it all and living solitary lives very soon after the death of Jesus Christ. Round about 350 AD, Christian hermits in the deserts of what is now called Saudi Arabia began to group together into small communities. Gradually, this idea spread until even remote islands, like Iona off the west coast of Scotland, had their own small communities of holy people. A man called Benedict, who lived in one of these small communities in Italy, began writing a series of rules about how such people should live.

WHAT WAS THE RULE OF ST BENEDICT?

St Benedict wrote his 'Little Rule for Beginners' some time between 535 and 547. These rules were so balanced and so sensible that they were gradually used by holy communities of men and women throughout Christendom. The Rule of St Benedict was really a complete guide to the organisation, running and well-being, both spiritual and material, of a monastery. Monasteries, nunneries, abbeys and priories that accepted the Rule of St Benedict expected their people to dedicate themselves to God by leading lives of poverty, obedience and chastity. Their days, except Sundays which were devoted entirely to worship, were divided into three parts: the hours of prayer and worship, the hours of study and the hours of work.

WERE ALL MONKS AND NUNS BENEDICTINES?

In 1066 all monasteries in Britain were Benedictine, lived in by monks and nuns who followed the Rule of St Benedict. Later, other Orders made more and sometimes different, rules. Apart from the Benedictines, the most important religious Orders in England were the Cistercians, the Carthusians and the Augustinians. There was, too, an Order that existed only in England – the Gilbertines.

Activity Time

Copy the grid below into your file or exercise book.
Research the four Orders, and complete the grid:

	CISTERCIANS	CARTHUSIANS	AUGUSTINIANS	GILBERTINES
When founded?	1098	1084	1104	
Where founded?	Citeaux, in Burgundy, France	French Alps		
Founded by whom?				
Based on whose Rule?		St Benedict	St Augustine	
Why founded?				
Men or women?	Men			Men and women
Known as?	White monks		Black Canons	
Special characteristics?		Each monk slept, ate, worked and prayed in his own room, meeting other monks only occasionally	Monks were all priests who worked outside the monasteries, taking services in parish churches, running schools, hospitals and almshouses	
Buildings in England?	Rievaulx Abbey, North Yorkshire	Mount Grace Priory, North Yorkshire		

WHAT WAS MONASTIC LIFE LIKE?

By 1300, there were over 700 religious communities in England operated by about ten different Orders. They all lived lives that were different in some ways and similar in others. However, the first duty of a monk or a nun was prayer. This never changed.

SOURCE 2

A painting of nuns praying in church, taken from a medieval manuscript.

SOURCE 3

Plan of Roche Abbey, South Yorkshire, in about 1350. The way in which a monastery was planned showed the importance of worship and prayer.

Question Time

Look carefully at the plan of Roche Abbey.

❶ How does it show that the monks placed great importance on prayer and worship?

❷ What does the plan tell you about what else the monks did and what was important to them?

❸ Look at the painting of nuns. How does it show the importance they placed on prayer and worship?

WHAT WAS A MONK'S DAILY ROUTINE?

In about 1350, when monastic life was at its peak, there were around 1000 religious houses and some 17,000 people (from a population of four million) living under religious vows. Different Orders lived in different ways. Roche Abbey was a large and well-organised Cistercian abbey. The table below tells you just how a choir monk there would have spent one of his days in about 1350.

Time of day	Activity	Place in abbey
2.00 hrs	VIGILS The Sacrist wakes the monks, who go down the night stairs to the church. The church service was performed in the dark from memory	Monks' choir in the church
3.30 hrs	Reading, prayers or meditation until dawn	Cloister or chapter house
Dawn	LAUDS A short church service	Monks' choir
6.00 hrs (approx)	PRIME A service said in the first hour of daylight, followed by High Mass	Monks' choir and High Altar
7.00 hrs	CHAPTER The monks assembled to hear holy readings, including some from the Rule of St Benedict. They confessed their sins and were disciplined. They discussed daily business and were given their daily duties. They then did manual work in the gardens and cloisters, workshops and kitchens	Chapter house Various places around the abbey
9.00 hrs	TERCE A short service followed by reading and meditation	The church and then the cloisters
11.30 hrs	SEXT A short service at the end of which the monks had a wash	The church and then the laver
12.00 hrs	PRANDIUM The main meal of the day, consisting of $2/3$ of the bread ration of 1lb, two dishes of boiled vegetables and watered wine or weak beer. Afterwards monks had a rest and then had a wash	The refectory and then the dormitory and laver
14.30 hrs	NONES A short service followed by a drink of water or wine and then more manual work	The church, the refectory and then around the abbey
17.30 hrs	VESPERS A church service	The church
18.00 hrs	The second meal of the day consisting of the remainder of the bread ration and fruit or salad. In winter, choir monks had only the one main meal	The refectory
18.30 hrs	COLLATION One monk read aloud to the others	Cloister or chapter house
20.00 hrs	COMPLINE The last service of the day. The monks then went to bed until woken at 2.00 hrs by the Sacrist	The church and then the dormitory

Question Time

Q

1 Work out how much of this monk's time was spent in prayer and worship, eating, working, sleeping.

2 Find out what lay brothers were, what they did and which Orders had lay brothers. How were lay brothers different from choir monks?

DID MONKS AND NUNS HAVE AN EASY LIFE?

Work through the following sources and make up your own mind!

SOURCE 4

Whenever anything important has to be decided, let the Abbot call together all the family. After hearing the advice of the brothers, let him make up his own mind. And let the brothers give their opinions humbly and presume not stiffly to argue for their own views. Prompt obedience is required of all monks. They live not as they themselves would choose but to be ruled by the Abbot.

The brothers are to serve each other so that no one be excused from the work of the kitchen. On Saturday he who ends his weekly kitchen work must clean up everything. He must wash the towels with which the brothers wash their hands and feet, and the person who is finishing his time in the kitchen and the person who is beginning it must wash the feet of the rest.

From the Rule of St Benedict.

SOURCE 5

These paintings are from illuminated manuscripts and show the sort of work a monk or nun had to do.

SOURCE 6

Excavations into a graveyard are giving us a glimpse of monastic life in twelfth-century Britain. The archaeologists have discovered that a life of prayer could be a hard one. One of the skeletons found showed signs of arthritis in the knees. Mr Currie, in charge of the dig, said this was 'hardly surprising for a monk who spends most of his life in a cold church on his knees.'

From *The Times* newspaper, 1987.

WHY DID MEN AND WOMEN BECOME MONKS AND NUNS?

Men became monks and women became nuns for many different reasons. The most basic and the most important reason of all was that they believed they needed to dedicate their lives to God and enter the monastic life. There were other reasons, too. There was the 'push' factor: things that they found wrong or disturbing or uncomfortable that made them want to change their ordinary, everyday lives for a monastic one. Then there was the 'pull' factor: things that they found attractive about the monastic life that made them want to enter it.

People could be hungry or very poor or one of a very large family where there was not a lot of anything to go round. A man might want to teach, or care for the sick, or illustrate manuscripts or write histories. A woman might be a widow or might not want to become a wife, but be looking for a fulfilling career. For all these people, the monastic life was very attractive. It offered a safe and secure home for life, together with food and clothing, companionship and

SOURCE 7

I am tormented and crushed down by the Vigils. I often yield to the manual labour. The rough clothing cuts through my skin. More than this, my will is always hankering after other things. It longs for the delights of the world and sighs for its pleasures.

Some monks clearly had a hard time!

SOURCE 8

When I was five years old, I was put to school in the town of Shrewsbury. There Siward, a priest, taught me my letters and instructed me in psalms and hymns. Then, O glorious God, you inspired my father to put me under your rule. So, weeping, he gave me, a weeping child, into the care of Reginald, and sent me away for love of you and never saw me again. And I obeyed him willingly for he promised me in your name that if I became a monk I should go to Heaven after my death.

Oderic Vitalis was ten years old when his parents decided he should become a monk. Fifty years later, he wrote about what happened.

SOURCE 9

Some specially skilled monks worked as chroniclers (writers of events and recent history), and sometimes painted beautiful little scenes inside large capital letters, or painted small pictures of everyday life in the margins and borders of the manuscripts. Much of what we know about medieval times comes from the history these monks have written. Monks and nuns copied out old and tatty manuscripts and in this way stopped learning from being lost.

a sense of purpose. It also offered a chance for men and women to develop particular skills. But life 'inside' wasn't easy and probably for most people the real force that took them into the monastic life and kept them there was the desire to serve God.

WHAT SORTS OF WORK DID MONKS AND NUNS DO?

Monks and nuns did a wide variety of work. Sometimes they specialised, for example, in copying and decorating manuscripts. Sometimes they were expected to turn their hands to anything: cooking, cleaning, digging and working in the fields. This varied according to the Order to which they belonged. Augustinians, for example, ran schools, hospitals and almshouses. Carthusians devoted themselves to prayer.

There were all sorts of different kinds of work to do with the running of monasteries and nunneries. The Abbot or Abbess was in charge and was responsible for all spiritual matters, orderly routine and discipline. The Cellarer ran the business side of things and was responsible for ordering supplies, paying the bills and keeping the accounts. The Kitchener was the catering officer, who ran the kitchens, ordered the food and supervised the cook and kitchen servants. The Sacristan was the security officer responsible for the plate, gold and silver in the abbey church as well as the tapers, candles and vestments. Not all monasteries and nunneries had people who worked at these particular jobs and some had people who did other things – like look after guests, sick people, the novices and all those who came begging for help of some kind.

SOURCE 10

These pictures show monks at a chapter meeting and chopping wood, both important parts of a monk or nun's life.

SOURCE 11

Monks and nuns were important in the treatment of the sick. As well as caring for sick monks and nuns, some monasteries and nunneries cared for local people, too. The Church set up hospitals, like St Bartholomew's, in London. There were not many of them, but they were well thought of by ordinary people. Not all hospitals had doctors and surgeons. Some were just for the care, not the treatment, of sick people. They provided clean and quiet surroundings, food, warmth and nursing care.

SOURCE 12

Some Orders encouraged their monks and nuns to teach. Often this involved teaching reading, writing and the Latin services to novices, young men and women who wanted to join their communities. Sometime this involved teaching ordinary men, women and children in the outside world.

Question Time

❶ The monk whose writing makes up Source 7 clearly felt he was hard done by! If the monastic life was harsh, why did people join at all?

❷ Choose one job done by a monk or a nun and make a list of everything you know about it. Now swap this list with the person sitting next to you.

❸ Read what your neighbour has written, and write down the questions you would like to ask about this job. Hand the paper back to your neighbour.

❹ Research and find answers to the questions about the job you chose. Remember to add all the information to your database.

WHY DID PEOPLE GO ON PILGRIMAGES?

WHAT IS A PILGRIMAGE?

A pilgrimage is a special journey to a place the people making the pilgrimage believe is holy. Today, some Christians make pilgrimages to Lourdes. This is a town in south-west France where, in 1858, a girl called Bernadette said she had seen the Virgin Mary, who was the mother of Jesus Christ. Each year, millions of people visit the grotto where Bernadette had her vision, because the spring there is said to have miraculous healing powers. Mecca is the most sacred of all Muslim cities because the prophet Muhammad, founder of Islam, was born there. Each year, during the Islamic month of Dhu al-Hija, around two million Muslims make a pilgrimage there. In medieval times, people also went on pilgrimages to their holy places.

WHO WENT ON PILGRIMAGES AND WHY?

All sorts of people went on pilgrimages in medieval times. Princes and priests, millers and butchers, stone-masons and master-gilders – all tried to make the effort and find the time and the money to go on a pilgrimage. They went for many different reasons. Some went to cure themselves from a dreadful illness, some went to speed themselves, or friends and relatives, through purgatory, others went to ask for a special favour or give thanks for something wonderful that had happened to them. Some went just for the fun of it and for something fashionable to do.

WHERE DID MEDIEVAL CHRISTIANS GO ON PILGRIMAGE?

The holiest place in the world for Christians was Jerusalem in the Holy Land where Jesus Christ was born, lived and was crucified. Next came Rome, where the Pope lived and had his cathedral called St Peter's. Christians hoped to be able to make a pilgrimage to either, or both, of these places,

This map shows where the main shrines were in England and Wales.

1 DURHAM CATHEDRAL
The shrine of St Cuthbert, a much-loved abbot of Lindisfarne and Bishop of Northumbria in the seventh century.

2 WALSINGHAM
in Norfolk, a famous statue of the Virgin Mary.

3 BURY ST EDMUNDS
in Suffolk. Tomb of King Edmund of East Anglia – killed by the Danes in the time of Alfred the Great.

4 ST ALBANS CATHEDRAL
Built on the hill where St Alban, the first christian martyr in England, was executed by the Romans in the third century, AD

5 WESTMINSTER ABBEY
Shrine of King Edward the Confessor – made a saint in the twelfth century.

6 CANTERBURY CATHEDRAL
Shrine of Archbishop Thomas Becket, murdered in 1170.

but obviously few could afford the time or the money to do so. Instead, most people tried to get to a holy place in their own country.

Pilgrims usually travelled in groups. This was partly for safety and partly so that they could support each other when the going got hard. Only the rich travelled on horseback. Most people simply walked. On some recognised pilgrim routes there were hostels where the travellers could stay. Otherwise, they had to rely on local inns or sleep rough.

WHAT MADE A LOCAL PLACE HOLY?

Most local holy places were shrines, which were often in a church or a cathedral. Shrines were places where relics were kept. A relic

SOURCE 1

Source 4 on page 94 told you about the priest.
This is what Chaucer wrote about some of the other pilgrims:

The Cook
You've stolen gravy out of many a stew
Many's the Jack of Dover you have sold
That has been twice warmed up and twice left cold;
Many a pilgrim's cursed you more than sparsely
When suffering the effects of your stale parsley
Which they had eaten with your stubble-fed goose;
Your shop is one where many a fly is loose.
Tell on, my gentle Roger, and I beg
You won't be angry if I pull your leg,
Many a true word has been said in jest.

The Miller
The Miller, very drunk and rather pale
Was straddled on his horse half-on half-off
'First I'm bound to say I'm drunk. I know it by my sound.
And if the words get muddled in my tale
Just put it down to too much Southwark ale.
There's many virtuous wives, all said and done,

Ever a thousand good for one that's bad.
One shouldn't be too inquisitive in life
Either about God's secrets or one's wife.
You'll find God's plenty all you could desire;
Of the remainder, better not enquire.'

The Franklin
A sanguine man, high-coloured and benign
He loved a morning sop of cake in wine.
He lived for pleasure and had always done ...
His bread, his wine, were finest of the fine
And no one had a better stock of wine.
His house was never short of bake-meat pies,
Of fish and flesh, and these in such supplies
It positively snowed with meat and drink
And all the dainties that a man could think.

The Doctor
The cause of every malady you'd got
He knew, and whether dry, cold, moist or hot.
All his apothecaries in a tribe

might be a saint's finger bone or a piece of cloth soaked with a saint's blood. There were other sorts of relics, too, and some of these were a bit dubious: wood from the cross on which Christ was crucified or a feather from an angel's wing, for example. But the important thing about all these relics was that people believed them to be holy and so made pilgrimages to where they could touch them or kneel before them.

GEOFFREY CHAUCER AND 'THE CANTERBURY TALES'

We know something about Geoffrey Chaucer's life, but there are some gaps and sometimes we have to make guesses. He was born around 1343, the son of a wealthy wine merchant. When Geoffrey Chaucer was a boy, he worked as a page in the household of King Richard II. By 1359, when he was about sixteen years old, he was fighting in the

Were ready with the drugs he would prescribe.
And each made money from the other's guile
They had been friendly for a goodish while.
In his own diet he observed some measure;
There were no superfluities for pleasure,
Only digestives, nutritives and such.
He did not read the Bible very much
Yet he was close as to expenses
And kept the gold he won in pestilences.
Gold stimulates the heart, or so we're told.
He therefore had a special love of gold

The Ploughman
Many a load of dung one time or other
He must have carted through the morning dew.
He was an honest worker, good and true,
Living in peace and perfect charity,
And, as the gospel bade him, so did he.
Loving God best with all his heart and mind
And then his neighbour as himself, repined
At no misfortune, slacked for no content,
For steadily about his work he went
To thrash his corn, to dig or to manure

Or make a ditch; and he would help the poor
For love of Christ and never take a penny
If he could help it, and, as prompt as any,
He paid his tithes in full when they were due
On what he owned, and on his earnings, too.

A wife from Bath
In making cloth she showed so great a bent
She bettered those of Ypres and of Ghent.
A worthy woman all her life, what's more
She'd had five husbands, all at the church door.
And she had thrice been to Jerusalem,
Seen many strange rivers and passed over them;
She'd been to Rome and also to Bologne,
St James of Compostela and Cologne.
She knew the remedies for love's mischances,
An art in which she knew the oldest dances.

Hundred Years' War. After that, he went on trade and diplomatic missions to Italy and France. He was a Customs Controller at the Port of London and a Clerk of Works at Westminster. We know that he married Philippa Roet, who worked at the royal court, and that they probably had two sons, called Lewis and Thomas.

WHY IS GEOFFREY CHAUCER IMPORTANT?

Chaucer isn't important for being a page, a diplomatist, a customs controller or a clerk of works. He is remembered for being a poet. The best-known poem is one he wrote in about 1386, called 'The Canterbury Tales'. It's about twelve people who are making a pilgrimage to the tomb of St Thomas Becket in Canterbury Cathedral.

Question Time

❶ Where did people go on pilgrimages? Could you guess where (a) the rich wool merchant living in Long Melford, Suffolk (b) the gate-keeper at Bamburgh castle, Northumberland and (c) the reeve on Cuxham manor, Oxfordshire went on pilgrimages near to them?

❷ Why did people go on pilgrimages? Use the sources and information in this section to help you in your answer. How can we be sure we know what people's real motives were?

❸ Read Source 1 carefully. Can we tell why these people went on pilgrimages?

❹ How helpful are Chaucer's writings to a historian wanting to find out about pilgrimages?

❺ What can we learn from Chaucer about life in medieval England?

❻ Find and read one of the murder mystery books by Ellis Peters featuring the twelfth-century Benedictine monk Cadfael as the detective.

WAS EVERYONE IN ENGLAND A CHRISTIAN?

Everyone in Britain was expected to be a Christian. They were expected to follow the teachings of the Church as to what they should believe and how they should behave. There was one exception to this: the Jews.

WHEN DID THE JEWS COME TO ENGLAND?

There were some Jews in England before 1066, but most settled in England after the Norman Conquest. Jews in Normandy had helped

William raise money for his invasion, and he encouraged them to come and settle in England afterwards. Indeed, the Jews were very useful to William and all the Norman kings. This was because, officially, Christians were not allowed by the Church to charge interest payments on any money they lent. This was known as usury. The Jews were not Christians and so were not bound by the same rules. They could lend money to anyone they chose, and make money themselves from the interest they charged.

WHERE DID THE JEWS LIVE?

Jews first settled in London in the area now known as Old Jewry, under the protection of the king. But by the time of King Stephen (1135-54), Jews were living in Norwich, Oxford, Cambridge and Winchester as well. One hundred years later they were living in towns as far apart as Exeter and York, Canterbury and Hereford. However, wherever the Jews were, they lived separately from their Christian neighbours. They usually lived in a particular street, or streets, close to the synagogue where they worshipped. Jewish customs and Talmudic law made Jews even more separate. They had their own laws relating to buying and selling property. Jewish communities had their own butchers, bailiffs and treasurers. Even in the king's courts, cases involving Jews were often decided by Jewish juries. It was this separateness that was later to make the Jews easy targets for persecution.

DID THE JEWS DO ANYTHING ELSE APART FROM LEND MONEY?

Jews could not swear a Christian oath to formalise a contract, so they could not own land or join a trade or craft guild. But they did run their own businesses and trades. Jews were, for example, wine merchants and fishmongers, cheese sellers and pawnbrokers, goldsmiths and doctors. However, most Jews made most of their money as money lenders. Many lent on a small scale, to craftsmen, shop keepers and students. Some wealthy Jews loaned money to kings and princes, burgesses and country gentlemen. They loaned money to the Catholic Church, too. For example, they made loans to the Abbot of St Albans, to the parish priests and canons of Lincoln and to the Archbishop of Canterbury. They helped fund the Crusades and the building of Fountains Abbey. People who were punished by a fine in the courts often went to Jewish money lenders for a loan.

WHY DID PEOPLE START PERSECUTING THE JEWS?

At first, Jews were protected by the kings to whom they lent enormous sums of money. The monarchs needed the loans and, besides, they taxed the Jews heavily, and they needed that money, too. Gradually, however, ordinary people began to resent the high interest they paid for borrowing Jewish money (usually between 2d and 3d per £1 borrowed, per week). Monarchs and other people wanted to find ways of getting out of making debt repayments. The Church, in debt to people it was supposed to despise for their role in crucifying Jesus Christ, needed to find a way out of the crippling interest it was paying. So the Church, the monarch and the people gradually turned on those from whom they had borrowed and on whom they had depended.

JEWS OUT?

There were a lot of different ways in which attitudes to the Jews changed until their situation in England became very difficult indeed.

First, there were rumours. Some people believed that Jews were killing Christian children. In 1144, an apprentice called William disappeared. He was found horribly murdered in Thorpe Wood, near Norwich. Rumours spread that he had been ritually killed by local Jews, although there was absolutely no evidence that any Jew had been involved in his death. The boy was buried in Norwich Cathedral and the Church encouraged people to regard William as something of a saint. Christians began taunting Jews and, in some towns and cities, rioted and burned Jewish houses, shops and other property. These disturbances started in London and spread to all other major cities where Jews lived. The ringleaders were townspeople and country gentlemen. Terrible violence occurred in York in 1190. Some Jewish families fled to York Castle for their own safety. A mob (whose leader owed the Jews a lot of money) surrounded the castle, chanting and jeering and demanding that the Jews become Christians. In desperation, fathers cut the throats of their wives and children to save them from this fate.

SOURCE 1

In their churches (synagogues) the Jews should worship in subdued tones, so that Christians hear it not and that no Christian man or woman serve any Jew or Jewess, nor eat with them nor dwell in their house and that every Jew wear on his breast a conspicuous badge. And that no Jew be received in any town without a special licence from the King, except in those towns where Jews have lived for a long time.

In 1253, Henry III published this law.

At daybreak, the mob leaders persuaded the few Jews left alive to leave the castle, and promptly killed them. The rioting ended with the townspeople making a giant bonfire of the records of loans made to them by Jews. Even in Winchester, where Jews and Christians got along well together, it was unsafe for a Jew to go out alone at night. Unjust laws made life even more difficult for the Jews.

Jews could not employ Christian servants and had to wear a special badge marking them out as Jews. Jews had to pay tithes to the priest of the local parish, just like Christians. But unlike Christians, they were not allowed to leave their belongings in the parish church for safety. All this made day-to-day living of Jews with their Christian neighbours more and more difficult. To many people, it seemed that the Church was agreeing with the ways in which the Jews were persecuted.

Throughout the thirteenth century, English kings taxed the Jews more and more heavily until most became poor and could pay no more.

After Edward I's law, the 2500-3000 Jews in Britain sold up what remained of their possessions, and left. They did not come back for nearly 400 years.

SOURCE 2

These enemies of the cross of Christ and blasphemers of the Christian faith, who impoverished Catholic folk by their usuries and compelled many of them thereby to sell their lands and possessions, should for ever depart.

In 1290, Edward I passed a law that affected Jews.

Question Time

1. Why did a lot of Jews come to England after 1066?

2. Why did they live in separate communities? Was it for Christian or Jewish reasons?

3. What important part did the Jews play in the lives of many people in medieval England?

4. Why did Edward I expel the Jews from England?

RUMBLINGS OF DISCONTENT?

Not everyone was happy with the ways in which the Church affected their lives and those of the people around them.

CRITICISMS OF MONKS, NUNS AND FRIARS

SOURCE 1

The Cistercians work so hard that they have become very rich, but they are mean and do not like to spend their wealth. They are happy to borrow farming equipment from others, but they will not lend anyone their ploughs. Their Rule does not allow them to work as parish priests, so when they are given new lands they destroy any villages there and throw out the people who live there.

The new Cistercian monks were not liked by everybody. Walter Map wrote this about them towards the end of the twelfth century.

SOURCE 2

When Samson became abbot, he spent a day of celebration with over a thousand dinner guests rejoicing greatly. As abbot he had several parks made for the abbey. He stocked them with wild animals and kept a huntsman and hounds. If an important guest was visiting, the abbot and his monks would sit in a clearing watching the hunt.

Jocelin of Brakelond wrote this about the Benedictine monastery of Bury St Edmunds at the beginning of the thirteenth century.

SOURCE 3

The friars go after the rich folk. They have no time for the poor. No one can be buried in one of their graveyards or churches unless he leaves them some money in his will.

From 'Piers Ploughman', written by William Langland in about 1380.

SOURCE 4

William Swinderby was a priest in Leicester. He said that people should not pay tithes to wicked, lazy or ignorant priests. The bishop was angry and banned him from preaching in churches. So he set up a pulpit in the street. Crowds from all over flocked to hear him.

A monk in Leicester, Henry Knighton, wrote this in 1390.

SOURCE 5

This painting of nuns going back to their abbey after a night of fun comes from a medieval manuscript.

JOHN WYCLIFFE AND THE LOLLARDS

John Wycliffe was a brilliant scholar who lectured at Oxford University from 1372 to 1382. He could say what he thought about the Church because he was protected by a great nobleman, John of Gaunt. John Wycliffe criticised the Church for two main reasons. Firstly, he said that its priests were often wealthy, ignorant and could not preach properly to the people. He urged monks and bishops to give up all their worldly possessions and lead simple lives. Secondly, he said that a person's belief should be based on the Bible alone, and not on what priests told them. It was therefore important that the Bible was translated from Latin (which not many people understood) into English, which everyone understood. The leaders of the Church disagreed. They said that only priests could understand the true meaning of the Bible and only they could explain it to the people. Wycliffe went further. He said there was no reason to believe the bread and wine used during the Mass changed into the flesh and blood of Christ; he said that there was no need for a Pope because Christ was the head of the Church.

By 1397, Wycliffe's followers had a good, clear translation of the Bible in English which they circulated throughout the country. Wycliffe's followers spread his ideas, and read from his Bible, in towns and villages throughout England. They were nicknamed 'Lollards' because people said they mumbled! Places like London, Bristol and Coventry soon had large Lollard communities. The Church had to act quickly. Lollards were arrested, tried before Church courts and thrown into prison. Some Lollards, who refused to change their ideas, were burned at the stake.

REFORM OR REFORMATION?

The Church managed to put down the Lollards, but it could not stop people thinking and questioning. It could not silence its opponents for ever. It could not stop people casting jealous eyes on the riches of the monasteries. It could not stop kings wanting to be the only power in their own lands.

Question Time

1 How reliable are Sources 1-5 as evidence of discontent with the Catholic Church?

2 Which groups of people were the greatest threat to the Catholic Church?

3 Is there enough evidence here to support the view that the Church needed reform?

HOW DID THE MEDIEVAL CHURCH AFFECT PEOPLE'S LIVES?

This is the question with which we started, and by now you should have a very good idea of the answer!

MAUD
the BREWER

Lives in a small village
Widowed with three children
Finds it hard to pay tithes
A grumbler

GARTH
the PIG-MAN

Works for a harsh lord of the manor
Unmarried and parents dead
Goes to church frequently
Always looks on the bright side

**JOHN
the SILVERSMITH**

Lives in a large town
Married with four children
Has been on a pilgrimage
A worrier

**CLARA
the BUSINESSWOMAN**

A successful businesswoman
Rich - Widowed twice
Gives to churches and monasteries
A careful planner

**DOMINIC
the FRIAR**

Preaches in markets and fairs
Unmarried
Does not want any possessions
Quietly hopeful

WILFRED the MONK

A Cistercian monk
Works as a cellarer
Helped make his monastery rich
Ambitious

Activity Time

Choose one of the characters above.

How would the person you have chosen answer the question,
'How has the Church affected your life?'

Use the relevant sources and information in this Unit to support
what you say.

Unit 5: Elizabeth 1 – how successfully did she tackle the problems of her reign?

WHY WAS RELIGION A LIFE OR DEATH PROBLEM IN ELIZABETHAN ENGLAND?

SOURCE 1

Campion with his fellow Jesuit Parsons visit England in 1580. What is his future? Look in the background for clues.

Raro antecedentem Scelestum:

Campian

F. Parfons et Campian

An artist's reconstruction of John Stubbs having his hand cut off.

WHY DID EDMUND CAMPION LOSE HIS LIFE?

Campion was a Jesuit priest who had fled abroad but returned to convert people back to being Catholic. Elizabeth's government spies caught him hiding in a house where he had said Mass. They put him on trial as a traitor, insisting that he was acting against his Queen, plotting against her and her religion (Protestantism). He insisted that he was just a religious man, but the law said that his religious beliefs were to do with politics and were therefore an act of treason. He was tortured and executed in 1581. More than one hundred other priests were also killed the same way, for the same reason.

JOHN STUBBS

The drawing at the bottom of page 120 shows a Puritan, John Stubbs, being punished by having his right hand chopped off. He had printed a book that criticised Elizabeth for considering marriage to a Catholic. He was a very strict Protestant, so Elizabeth was actually persecuting both Catholics and Protestants during her reign.

Which of the lines below do you think Stubbs was heard to say as soon as his punishment had been performed?

a) Long live Protestantism!
b) Long live the Puritans!
c) God save the Queen!

The answer is actually c. Does this make sense to you? Why would someone who had been sentenced and punished by Queen Elizabeth actually bless her name in public? Perhaps he wanted to impress Elizabeth.

The event shows the powerful influence of religion in this period – it really was a life or death matter. Problems over religion had existed since Henry VIII broke away from the Pope and the Catholic Church. Protestants and Catholics tortured and killed each other in this period. Elizabeth passed several Acts, in her 'Religious Settlement', which made the Church of England the official religion of the country. Most people were expected to be of the same religion as the monarch. To go against this was to be disloyal and a traitor. As we have seen, it could be dangerous. Also, in Elizabeth's reign you were fined if you did not go to church.

Religion in this period affected most aspects of life. We can see its influence in the churches that were built and also in the music, drama, poems and paintings that were created.

Question Time

1. Look at Source 1. How might a foreign chronicler, present at Edmund Campion's execution, have found out what was going on? What questions would he have had to ask the people watching the execution in order to find out?

2. Campion was loyal to Queen Elizabeth and had not stolen anything or murdered anyone. Have you any suggestions as to why then this man might have been executed?

3. What crime had Campion committed? Explain your answer carefully.

4. Why do you think that Stubbs called out this blessing?

5. What does this story tell us about the importance of (a) religion and (b) the power of the monarch in this period?

WHY WAS RELIGION SO IMPORTANT IN THE SIXTEENTH CENTURY?

- Religion affected every aspect of people's lives. God was the explanation for every event, whether good or bad.
- The chance of dying young was high as health care was not advanced. Belief in God and heaven meant that people had hope for their future.
- England was more strict about religion than the Middle East where religions other than Islam were still accepted in the sixteenth century.

Do any of these points still apply today?

WHY DID THE CONCEPTION OF ELIZABETH PRESENT A PROBLEM TO HER FATHER?

Elizabeth I's mother, Anne Boleyn, became pregnant in 1532. Henry VIII was in love with Anne, and he should have been delighted to be a father again with the possibility of getting a son at last. That would mean that the Tudor family would be safe on the throne of England in the future. However, Henry had several problems. First, he was still married to Catherine of Aragon. Catherine was 48 years old, and they had one daughter, Mary, but Catherine was unlikely to have any more children. Second, the Pope was unlikely to give Henry a divorce. After all, the Pope was influenced by the Emperor Charles V. Charles was Catherine's nephew and obviously would not support Henry divorcing his aunt. Henry was convinced that God was displeased with him. Catherine had been his brother Arthur's wife before he had died. Henry thought that his lack of a male heir was God's way of punishing him and he began to wonder whether he and Catherine were legally married. Henry's ministers tried to persuade the Pope to say that the marriage was invalid and grant a divorce. They were unsuccessful. But Henry needed this new child to be his real, legitimate heir. To do this he had to divorce Catherine and marry Anne. Ideas began floating into Henry's head. What if he could set up his own church?

SOURCE 1

If the pope is unwilling, we are left to find a cure elsewhere. Some cures are extreme ones, but a sick man looks for help in any way he can.

From a Letter to the Pope – signed by English lords and bishops in 1530.

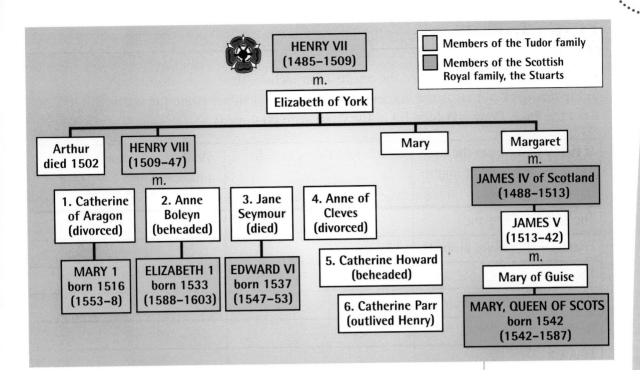

Members of the Tudor family

Members of the Scottish Royal family, the Stuarts

HENRY VII (1485–1509)
m.
Elizabeth of York

- **Arthur died 1502**
- **HENRY VIII (1509–47)** m.
- **Mary**
- **Margaret** m.

JAMES IV of Scotland (1488–1513)

JAMES V (1513–42) m.

1. **Catherine of Aragon (divorced)**
2. **Anne Boleyn (beheaded)**
3. **Jane Seymour (died)**
4. **Anne of Cleves (divorced)**

Mary of Guise

MARY 1 born 1516 (1553–8)
ELIZABETH 1 born 1533 (1588–1603)
EDWARD VI born 1537 (1547–53)

5. **Catherine Howard (beheaded)**

6. **Catherine Parr (outlived Henry)**

MARY, QUEEN OF SCOTS born 1542 (1542–1587)

OUT WITH THE POPE?

What did the Pope and being Catholic actually mean in England at this time?

- The Pope is the head of the Catholic Church, the most respected man in Europe.
- The Pope is in control of the entire Catholic Church. He makes all the main decisions, and benefits from the taxes, as people traditionally give some of their earnings to the Church.
- The Pope is the only person to grant divorces to Christians.
- Most people are Catholic and have worshipped in this way for centuries. Many Catholic traditions are very popular with people in England.
- Countries which are also Catholic could be natural allies (friends) with each other. This does not stop wars from taking place. England has fought with Catholic France and Spain a lot in the past. However, a country with a different religion is probably considered an enemy.
- The many monasteries in England are rich and powerful and own lots of land. They are Catholic and are a possible threat to Henry. If he splits with the Pope, he will have to take action against them as well.

Henry wanted to move away from being under the control of the Pope and the Catholic Church. But what would this mean for him and for England?

Question Time

1 Read Source 1. What do you think that this letter means when it mentions a 'cure'?

2 What is the general message to the Pope from the English lords and bishops?

3 Why would Henry want his bishops and lords to write to the Pope?

Question Time

The word 'consequences' means the results of an action. Using the information in the box work out what the consequences might be if Henry made the break from the Pope. Copy and then fill in the chart with your ideas.

If Henry broke from the Catholic Church what might happen to:	How might Henry benefit?	Would there be any problems?
The people in England?		
Friends and enemies abroad?		
The Pope?		
Henry's marriage and family?		
Henry's power?		
Money?		
Land?		

❶ Are there more benefits or problems on your consequences chart?

❷ Circle or colour in the two most important consequences on your chart. Compare your choices with the rest of the class.

❸ What action could Henry take? He could:

a stay Catholic and with Catherine of Aragon, hoping that she might have a boy.

b stay in the Catholic Church but hope that Anne Boleyn, his mistress, has a baby boy.

c break away from the Catholic Church, divorce Catherine and marry Anne.

What are the advantages and disadvantages of each of these alternatives?

HENRY'S BIG DECISION

At the marriage of Henry VIII and Anne Boleyn, Anne was obviously pregnant and was booed at by the crowds. Did Henry mind? He certainly got his own way. He broke away from the Pope, set up his own church, granted his own divorce and then married Anne. In giving himself the title of 'Head of the Church of England' Henry introduced one of the most important changes in this country's history. It changed religious history, led to years of problems and gave the monarchy of England far more power. What was going on? Was it all to do with Anne Boleyn?

WHAT CAUSED THE REFORMATION?

The changing of the official religion in England is called the English Reformation. The word 'Reformation' means a great change, usually for the better. Henry VIII started the Reformation, although it actually took several decades. Why did it happen?

The corrupt Church

The Catholic Church had been criticised for some years. People like John Wycliffe (1320–84) and Martin Luther (1483–1546) argued that it was too rich and powerful. Monks in particular had moved away from their original aims of worshipping God and leading a simple, humble life. Monks were accused of corruption, having wives, not taking sacred vows seriously, gambling, drinking and being far too wealthy.

Popular Protestantism

Ideas about an new type of Christianity spread across Europe. In Germany Martin Luther protested that people did not need the Catholic Church in order to get to heaven. They should just believe in God and Jesus and learn about Christianity from the Bible. This started Protestantism, from the word 'protest'. Some monarchs became Protestant, as it made religious sense. Others could see the advantages of breaking away from the powerful control of the Catholic Church. Germany, Switzerland and the Netherlands all became Protestant by the 1540s. Many people were unhappy with the Catholic Church anyway, so these new, simple ideas about religion were very attractive.

Money matters

Henry VIII wanted to increase his personal power and the reputation of England in Europe. One obvious way was to go to war. It also kept his barons busy and out of trouble. He had recently fought against France and Scotland at the same time. But wars cost money. So did Henry's luxurious lifestyle. He needed his ministers to raise more cash.

People power

Thomas Cromwell was Henry's main adviser. He was a clever man, and he knew that he had to please the king or risk his job and his life. Henry's former minister, Wolsey, was already charged with treason. Cromwell and the Archbishop of Canterbury, Cranmer, advised Henry on religious and political affairs. They told him that he could be head of his own church and grant his own divorce. This was just what Henry wanted to hear.

Baby boom

In 1532 Anne Boleyn became pregnant. This meant that if Henry could marry her he might be able to have a son, a strong heir to the throne. He had been trying to divorce Catherine for several years, but the pope would not agree. Now he had a stronger reason. He needed a divorce and needed his ministers to say that his marriage to Catherine had not been a real one. This would mean that people would accept Anne as his wife and recognise their child as his legitimate heir.

Question Time

Can you understand exactly how each of these factors led to the Reformation in England?

1 Match three of the factors to their correct explanation. Write out both halves to make a full sentence:

The new ideas in religion

meant that many people did not trust Catholicism as much

The problems with the Catholic Church

which meant that he did not have to make the decision alone

Henry was advised to set up his own church

this meant that some people were keen to introduce Protestantism

2 Explain the effects of the other two factors yourself. Use words/phrases like 'because', 'and so' and 'this meant that' to help you to explain.

3 Can you think of any other reasons? Look back at pages 122–126. We can make a diagram out of these different reasons to help us to understand them. Design a flow diagram and label and describe each of the types of reasons below on your diagram. You may need to plan it in rough first.

  a long-term reasons (had been present for a while)

  b short-term reasons (more recent in time)

  c a trigger (something that sparked Henry into action)

  d the most important reasons in big boxes, the less important ones in small boxes

  e any connections between different causes – draw arrows to show the connection.

4 Historians disagree about which of these causes is most important. Some historians say that the Reformation would have happened anyway. Compare your diagram with others in your group. Discuss:

  a What is the same?

  b What is different?

  c What is it hard to agree on?

  d Why do you think this is?

5 As a class, try to agree on which factors are long term, short term, a trigger and most/least important and make one giant diagram to sum up all the reasons for Henry's break from the Catholic Church. You could even research to find out if there are any other reasons that you could add. Each person should be responsible for labelling or explaining one reason.

THE LAST LAUGH

How do you think that Henry VIII felt when he heard that Anne had given birth to a healthy baby girl?

WHAT RELIGIOUS CHANGES WERE TAKING PLACE IN THE REST OF EUROPE?

EARLY COMPLAINTS

As long ago as 100 years before Henry VIII broke away from the Pope, people had begun to complain about the Catholic Church. John Wycliffe argued that the church was too rich and powerful, but this idea did not become fashionable until the 1500s. In 1516 a man called Erasmus said that ordinary people should be able to understand the Bible for themselves and this meant translating it from Latin into the languages the people spoke. People slowly began to question whether the Catholic Church should begin to change.

MARTIN LUTHER COMPLAINS IN STYLE

In 1517 a Catholic priest, Martin Luther, from Germany decided that he had had enough of the corruption of the Catholic Church.

LUTHER'S TOP COMPLAINTS (OUT OF 95!)

1 People should not have to speak to God through a priest.
2 Faith is enough to make people lead good lives and so get to heaven.
3 Going on pilgrimages and to Mass is not as important as believing in Jesus Christ.
4 People cannot read the Bible for themselves as it is written in Latin.
5 The Pope should not be the overall ruler of every country.
6 It is only God who forgives people's sins. Indulgences (buying a pardon for sins from a priest) are wrong.

Martin Luther went to his local church in Wittenberg and nailed a huge list of complaints to the front door. He could not fail to be noticed. In the list he complained about many aspects of the Church.

Luther said that the Bible had told him that belief in God and Jesus was enough to make someone a Christian. Forgiveness and a way into heaven could not be earned or bought.

Luther also later criticised the massive wealth and power of the Church. He was ordered to go and explain himself to the Emperor. How dare a simple priest make so many complaints?

Question Time

1. What would Luther's criticisms mean for
   a the Catholic Church
   b his reputation as a Catholic priest?

2. In pairs, turn Luther's top six criticisms into suggested changes that the Catholic Church should make, by rewriting them. For example, number one could be 'teach people to pray to God for themselves'.

3. Which suggestions do you think are the most important? Explain your answer to the rest of the class.

4. Which suggestion do you think would be the most unpopular with:
   a the Pope
   b Catholic priests in Germany
   c German Catholics (local people)?

PROTESTANTISM SPREADS ACROSS EUROPE

Popular with the people. Although a few other people like Wycliffe had criticised the Catholic Church before Luther and even begun to translate bibles into other languages, Luther really made a difference. Along with John Calvin, who preached even more extreme ideas, Luther introduced Protestantism into Europe. They gave people a list of ideas to agree and disagree with. People interpreted Luther's ideas in different ways, so there were actually different types of Protestantism in different countries, but they all had similar beliefs about Christianity.

Popular with the princes and kings. There were several reasons that princes and leaders were keen to accept Luther's ideas and break away from the Catholic Church.

The Catholic Church excommunicated (expelled) him but Luther showed that he did not care by burning the excommunication letter that he had received from the pope.

People began to listen to Luther and his ideas caught on. They were spread across Europe by the invention of the new printing presses.

Luther's new ideas about religion formed the start of Protestantism. The movement became too strong for the Church to stop and spread quickly across parts of Europe.

Many leaders liked the idea of the independence that a move away from the Church would bring. Others thought of the amount of taxes they could claim instead of the money going to the Church. Others believed that the Church needed to reform (change for the better) and believed strongly in Martin Luther's ideas. For some monarchs, it was a mixture of all three reasons.

HOW SUCCESSFUL WAS THE SPREAD OF PROTESTANTISM?

The Catholic Church felt threatened by the popularity of Protestantism and started its own 'Counter Reformation'. This meant that Protestants were hunted down and put on trial for heresy (believing in ideas against a religion). People were fined and excommunicated (expelled from the Church). Others were tortured, imprisoned or even burned to death.

Question Time

1 Would you say that the spread of Protestantism was more successful in northern Europe than in southern Europe?

2 Can you think of three reasons why Protestantism was so popular?

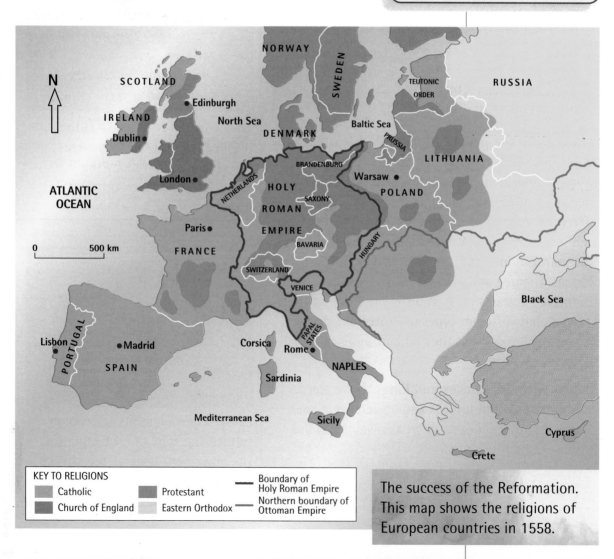

KEY TO RELIGIONS

Catholic	Protestant
Church of England	Eastern Orthodox

— Boundary of Holy Roman Empire
— Northern boundary of Ottoman Empire

The success of the Reformation. This map shows the religions of European countries in 1558.

WHAT DID ELIZABETH DO ABOUT THE RELIGIOUS PROBLEM IN ENGLAND?

After Henry VIII had introduced the Reformation in England, the speed of religious change slowed down. He made himself head of the Church, divorced Catherine and married Anne, but he did not make many actual changes to what went on in churches across the country. Later, his son and heir Edward, who was brought up as a strict Protestant, was keen to change the way that people worshipped. When Edward died at the age of fifteen, having been king for just six years, his elder sister, Mary, became queen. She had been brought up a strong Catholic, and she followed her beliefs to change the religion of the country back to Catholicism. During Mary's reign nearly 300 Protestants were burned to death for refusing to turn their backs on their new religion. So, by the time Elizabeth became queen, the country had had enough of religious arguments. Elizabeth wanted to rule over a peaceful England. But it was not that easy...

SOURCE 1

Holy bread and holy water was given, altars redecorated, pictures put up, the cross and a crucifix ready to be carried in processions. All the English service lately used in the church was put away and the Latin taken up.

A Yorkshire man's view of Mary's reign, from the *Narrative of Robert Parkyn*.

SOURCE 2

The 5th day after in September (1547) began the King's visit to St Paul's, and all the images were pulled down; and the 9th day after of that same month the visit was to St Bride's, and after that to other churches; and so all images were pulled down in England at that time, and all churches painted with new whitewash, with the Commandments written on the walls.

A description of London in the reign of Edward VI, from the *Chronicle of Grey Friars*.

The churches chart

	Catholic churches and church services	Protestant churches and church services	Churches and services under Elizabeth I
Decoration of building	• wall-paintings •		
Layout of building			
Priests/ministers		• wear plain gowns	
Language used		• English Prayer Book	
Style of services			

Interior of a church in Edward's reign.

plain glass in window

plain cross

Bible (in English)

plain table

white-washed walls

priest with simple robes

Interior of a Catholic church in Mary's reign.

rood screen

crucifix

ornate altar cloth

paintings on walls

altar boy with incense

priest with ornate robes

stained glass window

ELIZABETH'S RELIGIOUS CHANGES

Elizabeth wanted everyone to follow the same religion in England to keep the country at peace. She was Protestant, but she knew that if the Protestantism practised in the English churches was too extreme, she would be unpopular with the many Catholics in the country. She also knew that if she let the country become more Catholic, she would upset the Protestants. Elizabeth's religious policy was a balancing act of keeping all religious groups happy. She got Parliament to pass a Religious Settlement to make the Protestant religion law, with her as its 'governor'.

Question Time

❶ Look at Sources 1 and 2 and the drawings on this page. Copy and complete the first two columns of the chart on page 131 to show what Catholic and Protestant churches were like in this period. Find some extra points for the chart by researching in the school library, on the Internet or in an encyclopaedia. Using the information above and your own research, fill in the last column on your churches chart to show what religion was like in Elizabeth's reign.

John Knox, a Scottish Protestant, said that Elizabeth and her Church was 'neither good Protestant, nor yet a Catholic'.

❷ What do you think he meant by this?

❸ Do you agree? Explain both answers as much as you can using ideas from your churches chart.

Factfile: Elizabeth's religious changes

- Elizabeth's religious laws are called her Religious Settlement.

- By 1563 Elizabeth's Parliament had passed several laws to make sure that everyone accepted her as the proper monarch of England, in charge of the Church.

- The laws also made sure that everyone used the same Prayer Book and agreed on the basic ideas of the Church of England.

- The Settlement included rules to make sure that priests wore the old-style vestments (gowns) and that every church should use an English Bible.

- It upset some Protestants who thought that there was too much of the old Catholic religion in the services and traditions that were kept.

- Although there was a serious rebellion in 1569 (the Rebellion of the Northern Earls) most people followed Elizabeth's Religious Settlement and there were no uprisings or open protests.

SOURCE 3

At first even those who had been Catholic did not see any great change from the old religion in the new set up by Queen Elizabeth, apart from the different language (changed to English).

The view of a lawyer from Monmouthshire, who later became a Catholic monk.

ELIZABETH'S RELIGIOUS ENEMIES

Elizabeth's policy of trying to keep people happy, as long as they stayed loyal, worked up to a point. She did have religious enemies, but as we have seen on pages 120-121, being Elizabeth's enemy could be a dangerous business. Two of the groups who disagreed with her Religious Settlement were the Jesuits and the Puritans (see page 134). Work out why they disagreed with her. Did they have the same ideas?

I am a Jesuit priest. The Jesuit Society was set up in 1543. We work for the Pope to protect the Catholic religion against the heretics (people who go against the true Catholic faith). The people who are spreading these dangerous ideas should be caught and punished. We are highly trained and educated priests, dedicated to our mission. We spread the teachings of the true Church and hunt out troublemakers, forcing them to see how wrong they are. We believe in the traditional ways of the Catholic Church. We want to protect old-style services and the Mass in Latin. The influence of bishops and priests is important and the Pope is God's leader of the Church on earth.

Puritans have no time for the old ways of the corrupt Catholic Church. We believe that people do not have to worship in a certain way, using a Prayer Book with a special priest as leader. People can speak to God on their own and through reading the Bible. Our leaders are chosen by ourselves; we are all equal. They do not have any privileges or special power. The old Catholic rituals like singing Latin mass, music from organs or wearing decorated vestments (clothes worn by priests) just take people's mind away from God. We do not need decoration in our churches, just ourselves, a Bible and God.

Question Time

Work out why the Jesuit and the Puritan are so unhappy at Elizabeth's religious policy. Write your own speech bubble for each of them explaining what they don't like about Elizabeth's Religious Settlement. Include examples of their complaints.

WERE CATHOLICS OR PURITANS THE GREATER THREAT TO ELIZABETH'S RELIGIOUS SETTLEMENT?

Read all about it!

Fines increased for not going to church

Jesuit Campion hung, drawn and quartered for treason

Puritan Stubbs' hand cut off

100 priests executed for challenging Elizabeth

These headlines are all describing events under Elizabeth's reign. Which of them do you think are true? You have already learned about what happened to Edmund Campion and John Stubbs, but all the other headlines are also events that really happened.

Although the majority of people in England accepted Elizabeth's Religious Settlement, there were religious groups who did not. The two largest groups were the Catholics and the Puritans. You have already seen how different they were in their beliefs, but both groups were strong opponents of Elizabeth and they also had contacts abroad. Remember that as a female monarch, with no husband or son and heir, Elizabeth could not be too careful. She had to guard against trouble from both England and abroad.

HOW SERIOUS A THREAT WERE THE CATHOLICS?

In 1570 Elizabeth was excommunicated by the Pope. This meant that she was expelled from the Catholic Church and the Pope declared that she was not the rightful leader of the Church or the country. Catholics were told that they did not have to obey her orders. This could have serious consequences for Elizabeth.

DETERMINED CATHOLICS

Most Catholics were happy to accept Elizabeth as their monarch and just believe in Catholicism in their hearts. Some, however, were more determined that the old religion should not be abandoned. The Pope obviously agreed. He sent Jesuit priests to England to spread Catholicism. The priests were smuggled into the country and hidden by rich Catholic families in their large country houses. They acted as their private priests, holding secret Masses in Latin for them and their Catholic friends. But they had to be careful. In the 1580s Elizabeth became especially worried about the Catholic threat to her country. Relations with Spain were not good and she had already discovered several Catholic plots against her. She was concerned as so many Catholics had contacts with France and Spain, her enemies.

ELIZABETH TAKES ACTION

Elizabeth's parliaments passed a series of laws against Catholics. Fines were increased for not going to church. This forced many poorer Catholics back to the Church of England but Elizabeth knew that the wealthy families were not really affected. She sent soldiers to search their homes for Catholic priests. Many country houses in England, such as Moseley Old Hall in Staffordshire, had secret cupboards and passages, called priest holes, that would have hidden Catholic priests from the government. Catholic priests could be imprisoned, tortured or executed for treason since they did not accept Elizabeth as the ruler of England and the leader of its new Church. Elizabeth's clever minister Walsingham set up a huge spy network. People would keep watch on their neighbours, their friends, servants and employers. In this way he managed to track down over 100 Catholic priests. They were dealt with harshly.

SOURCE 1

Elizabeth, the pretended Queen of England, the servant of wickedness has helped many heretics. This very woman has taken the country and ruined it, which was so healthy recently under the Catholic religion. She should be cut off from the Church and deprived of all her power. Her subjects (people) are freed from obeying her on any matter.

An extract from the Papal Bull of 1570 in which the Pope excommunicated Elizabeth.

SOURCE 2

A painting showing Catholic priests who are about to be hanged. When they are still alive they will be quartered (cut into four pieces).

SOURCE 3

There are many people in the realm (country) that differ in some opinions of religion from the Church of England, but they do also stay loyal and obedient to Her Majesty. None of these are charged with any crimes of treason.

Lord Burghley, one of Elizabeth's most trusted ministers, explaining how many Catholics are safe in England.

HOW SERIOUS A THREAT WERE THE PURITANS?

How were the Puritans a threat to Elizabeth? After all, they were not connected to the Spanish or French and they did accept Elizabeth as the proper Queen of England. However, many MPs were Puritan and their beliefs did challenge Elizabeth in a way. They disagreed with her Religious Settlement and so challenged her authority in England. Many MPs criticised Elizabeth in Parliament, saying that the Church of England was not Protestant enough. Some MPs campaigned for a new prayer book to be published but Elizabeth ignored their demands. She was happy with the Religious Settlement and knew that any changes in favour of the Puritans would upset the Catholics. The Puritan threat faded away for Elizabeth but was to return in the next century.

Question Time

1 What do the headlines on page 135 tell us about religion under Elizabeth's rule?

2 What reasons does the Pope give in Source 1 for excommunicating Elizabeth?

3 What could the message in Source 1 mean for Catholics in England?

4 Look at Source 2. Why would both (a) Catholics and (b) Protestants probably want to draw pictures of these priests being hanged, drawn and quartered?

5 Who did Elizabeth consider as more of a threat:
a poor working Catholics?
b wealthy Catholic families?
c Jesuit priests from abroad?
Explain your answer fully.

6 a How do you think a Catholic landowner in the north of England would have reacted to a request for him to give a Jesuit priest shelter in his household?
b What action might he take to protect himself?

SOURCE 4

Their feast days, may-games, sports, plays and shows led people away from the fear of God. The days set forth for holy days were usually the times when they most dishonoured God by those things.

George Fox, a Puritan, complaining about activities on holy days such as Sundays.

SOURCE 5

At the beginning they argued over just a hat or a surplice (gown that priests wear). Now it has grown to bishops, archbishops, to overthrowing the established order. These men would not only have equality of all ministers but would deprive the Queen of her authority and give it to the people.

The Dean of York warning Lord Burghley about the challenge of the Puritans to the Queen's power during Elizabeth's reign.

SOURCE 6

All priests must accept:
- *Elizabeth's authority as Queen*
- *that they will use only the Book of Common Prayer in services*
- *the basic ideas about religion set down in the Religious Settlement.*

Elizabeth's Archbishop of Canterbury, Whitgift, passed the Three Articles in 1583. All priests had to accept these basic ideas or they could be thrown out of the Church. They were forced to make a decision one way or the other.

Question Time

As we saw on pages 120 and 121 Elizabeth dealt harshly with the Puritans as well as the Catholics.

Who do you think posed Elizabeth the greater threat? Compare the areas below for both groups, find some more evidence and hold a debate or class discussion to find an answer.
- Foreign contacts
- Obedience to the Queen
- Criticisms of her ideas
- Support from the people
- Ability of Elizabeth and her ministers to maintain control.

Activity Time

Design a poster to show how the Puritans wanted people to behave. Mention what they hated about the Church of England, but be careful not to criticise Elizabeth too much – it could be dangerous.

WHY DID MARY, QUEEN OF SCOTS, POSE SUCH A BIG PROBLEM FOR THE QUEEN?

By 1563 Elizabeth had introduced her Religious Settlement and had solved the biggest religious problems. However, her reign was not free from trouble. In the 1580s a series of plots against Elizabeth were discovered. They ended with serious consequences, one of which Elizabeth possibly regretted for the rest of her life.

SOURCE 1

A painting of the execution of Mary, Queen of Scots, 1587.

Picture the scene. After months of worry and indecision Elizabeth reluctantly agreed to sign an important piece of paper. It was a death warrant to execute a prisoner. Elizabeth convinced herself that the action was correct – after all the Court had found the prisoner guilty. The messenger quickly took the news to Fotheringay Castle where the prisoner was held...

The prisoner took off her cloak as she moved towards the block. The crowd gazed at her bright scarlet dress and wondered whether she had worn this deliberately in defiance. She stepped forward, praying aloud in Latin as she knelt down. A woman gave her some dignity by placing a cloth over her face and pinning it in place. It took two blows of the axe to remove her head. After the first blow the prisoner could be heard to make no noise.

Factfile: Mary, Queen of Scots

Mary in France – a princess and a queen

- Mary became Queen of Scotland as a baby, but she was brought up as a Catholic in her mother's home, France. This was to make sure that she was safe as England and Scotland were at war.
- Mary married Francis, the French prince and later became his queen. She enjoyed life at the French court and hardly spoke a word of Scottish or English.
- When Francis died in 1560, Mary returned to Scotland as queen.

Mary in Scotland – a Catholic queen and foolish woman

- Mary was not popular in Scotland. The country was now Protestant and Mary was still a strict Catholic. But she also made mistakes and lost the trust of her nobles.
- First, she married the handsome, but dangerous, Catholic Lord Darnley. The marriage was not successful and Darnley showed his true character by having Mary's secretary, Rizzio, killed in front of her. He was stabbed over 50 times.
- Then Darnley himself was killed. His home at Kirk o' Field was blown up and he was found strangled in the grounds.
- Mary's new 'friend' James, Earl of Bothwell was suspected of the murder. When Mary married him soon after it seemed to confirm that Bothwell, and possibly Mary, had in fact killed Darnley. The Scottish nobles had had enough. Not only was their queen a Catholic, but she could not be trusted.
- Mary was chased out of Scotland, and her baby son, James, became King James VI of Scotland.

Mary in England – a prisoner and a troublemaker?

- Mary went to her cousin Elizabeth for help.
- Elizabeth was in a difficult situation. Mary was her cousin and her nearest relative. But Mary had always made it clear that she thought that she had the true claim to the English throne. Elizabeth did not know if she could trust her.
- Mary was imprisoned in various country houses in England.
- Parliament unsuccessfully tried to persuade Elizabeth to have Mary executed for treason.
- Mary was a focus for any Catholic group who wanted to remove Elizabeth from the throne.

After the second fall of the axe the executioner held up the head for everyone to see. The crowd was shocked to see the grey hair of the prisoner as her hair piece fell to the ground. After all, she was only 45 years old. A small scared dog ran out from underneath the skirts of the body, but it would not leave her.

When news of the execution reached Elizabeth, she was stunned. She screamed, shouted and demanded answers. She had not meant this to happen. After all, the prisoner was her cousin, Mary, Queen of Scots. She would live with this guilt for the rest of her life.

This is an amazing true story.

DECISION TIME – YOU BE THE JUDGE

The problem: what to do with Mary, Queen of Scots? She is a focus for troublemakers and Catholic plotters. Elizabeth's problems are that not only is Mary her cousin, but she is also a queen. However, as a Catholic she could ally (take sides) with other Catholic countries and plot against England. To make matters worse, relations with Catholic Spain were becoming tense. Although Mary was closer to France, Spain's enemy, Elizabeth could not really be sure that Mary would not get help from Spain for her cause.

Vital information: the Catholic plots. In the space of 15 years, there were a series of Catholic plots against Elizabeth. Walsingham's spies managed to find the culprits, but they reminded Elizabeth of the threat that remained as long as Mary was still alive. Mary's or her supporters' involvement in these plots was suspected but nothing had been proved.

Question Time

1 Make a list of questions that you want to ask about what happened to Mary Queen of Scots.

2 What questions does the family tree on page 123 answer?

3 What other questions does it raise?

An important question is why would one cousin be involved in the killing of another? In order to answer this, we need to find out more about the life of the prisoner, Mary, Queen of Scots.

4 Why did Elizabeth and Mary become enemies? Think of religion and Mary's claim to the English throne in your answer.

SOURCE 2

She has challenged the crown of England. She has made the Duke of Norfolk disobedient to your Majesty. She has stirred the Duke of Northumberland and Westmorland to rebel. We, your true and obedient servants, do most humbly ask your Majesty to punish and correct all these treasons.

Parliament brought charges against Mary, Queen of Scots, as early as 1572.

SOURCE 3

A painting of Mary, Queen of Scots in 1578. The caption says that she is Queen of Scotland, widow of the King of France, 36 years old and captured in England.

MARIA
D   G
SCOTIÆ
PIISSIMA REGINA
FRANCIÆ DOTARIA
ANNO
ÆTATIS REGNIQ
36
ANGLICÆ CAPTIVIT
10
5   H
1578

WAS MARY INVOLVED IN THE BABINGTON PLOT TO KILL ELIZABETH?

People suspected that Mary had been involved in earlier plots against Elizabeth's life, but in 1586 Elizabeth's ministers finally had some proof of her secret deals.

- While locked up, Mary received letters from a Catholic called Anthony Babington. The letters were hidden in beer barrels and smuggled in and out of the castle. Babington wanted to kill Elizabeth and, with the support of Catholic armies from Europe, put Mary on to the throne in her place.

- Mary replied to Babington saying that she would follow his plans.

- Walsingham, Elizabeth's spymaster, discovered all the letters and now had proof that Mary was plotting against Elizabeth.

- It has been suggested that one of Walsingham's spies had forged Mary's comments to Babington, in the hope that she would be caught and executed.

- Mary was put on trial for her part in the Babington Plot but the Court could not prove that the handwriting was Mary's.

- The Court found Mary guilty of treason.

Activity Time

Sort out the evidence listed on pages 141 and 142 into two columns in a chart to show whether Mary was innocent or guilty.

Mary is guilty	Mary is innocent

Your options:

   a) set Mary free as long as she goes abroad,
   b) keep her locked up forever,
   c) have her executed for treason.

You are a member of the Privy Council in England in 1587. You have carried out an investigation into the possible guilt of Mary, Queen of Scots. Write a report to Elizabeth advising her whether Mary should be executed or not. Include these headings:

- Was Mary really involved in the plot – evidence from her past and from her years as a prisoner

- Other evidence against her

- Evidence to support Mary

- The results if she lives

- The results if she dies

- What other options are possible and any problems with these

- Your suggested action.

Remember that your report must be based on the attitudes that existed in 1587.

Question Time

❶ Look back at the Factfile on Mary. How much can we tell about her character and her wisdom as a ruler?

❷ Look at the portrait, Source 3. How does the artist makes Mary look like a strong and religious woman and also a victim?

❸ Why would the pope's excommunication of Elizabeth in 1570 make the Catholic threat even worse?

❹ Why do you think that Elizabeth did not execute Mary when Parliament asked her to in 1572?

WHY DID PHILIP OF SPAIN POSE SUCH A BIG PROBLEM FOR ELIZABETH I?

PHILIP II OF SPAIN – FRIEND OR ENEMY?

Philip II of Spain was Elizabeth's brother-in-law. But Mary I was dead and Philip was the King of Spain, one of the most powerful men in Europe. When she became queen, Elizabeth considered Philip's offer of marriage. By 1585 they were at war against each other. What had gone wrong with their relationship?

TIMELINE OF EVENTS – THE STEPS TO WAR

1559 – Philip proposes marriage to Elizabeth when she becomes queen. He had been married to her half-sister Mary for the four years before she died.

1569 – Elizabeth considering marriage to Duke of Alençon. He is the heir to the French throne and Philip's enemy.

1570 – Francis Drake raids Spanish ships and takes South American treasure back to Elizabeth.

1570 – Elizabeth is excommunicated by the Pope.

1585 – Elizabeth sends the Earl of Leicester and an army to the Netherlands to help Protestant rebels who are fighting against Philip.

1587 – Drake 'singes the beard' of Philip by raiding Cadiz and destroying 30 royal warships and ships carrying supplies ready to invade England.

1587 – Elizabeth executes Mary, Queen of Scots. Philip is furious. His hope of bringing back Catholicism is set back.

1588 – Philip sends 130 ships to invade England and remove Elizabeth from the throne, but the Armada fails (see page 145).

1559
1560
1561
1562
1563
1564
1565
1566
1567
1568
1569
1570
1571
1572
1573
1574
1575
1576
1577
1578
1579
1580
1581
1582
1583
1584
1585
1586
1587
1588

Activity Time

① Draw a graph like the one below to plot how Elizabeth and Philip's relationship changed over the years. Label each of the main events from the timeline along the bottom of the graph. Put a cross to show how the relationship between Elizabeth and Philip changed – was it good or bad, or even very bad. One example has been done for you.

② Go back to your graph of Elizabeth and Philip's relationship. Label each event or cross to see whether it was to do with **(a)** personal life **(b)** religion **(c)** money **(d)** power and politics. You could design a symbol for each type of event, for example a heart for the personal life. Don't forget to add a key.

③ Now use your graph to explain why their relationship went from good to bad. Include ideas about religion, the threat to the English throne and other countries in your answer. Say what you think was the most important type of reason for the change in relationship between Elizabeth and Philip.

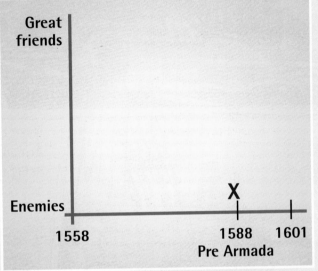

FIGHTING THE SPANISH – THE ARMADA

By 1588 relations with Philip II had become desperate. Spain was one of the strongest countries in Europe in the sixteenth century. When a huge Spanish fleet sailed towards England ready to invade, many people expected it to be successful. So why did it fail and return to Spain without even landing on the coast of England?

THE BACKGROUND

Elizabeth became queen, refused to marry Philip and was excommunicated by the Pope. You have studied the other reasons why England and Spain became enemies on page 144.

In 1587 the Pope commented on Elizabeth: 'What a valiant (brave) woman! She braves the two greatest kings by land and sea.' Was the defeat of the Armada really down to Elizabeth's courage in facing the Spanish? See what you think.

THE SPANISH FLEET LEAVES SPAIN FOR ENGLAND

Delayed start to invasion as Drake had destroyed many ships and supplies in his raid on Cadiz.

Duke of Medina Sidonia put in charge of the Armada was sea sick and hated the job. Spanish delay meant that English were well prepared.

The Spanish were attacked by English fireships in the Channel – Spanish panicked, cut their anchors and separated. The Spanish fleet was also blown off course by a rough storm. They were separated and then attacked by the English using cannons. Fifty English sailors were killed, but no ships were lost. The Spanish lost three ships and over 1000 men.

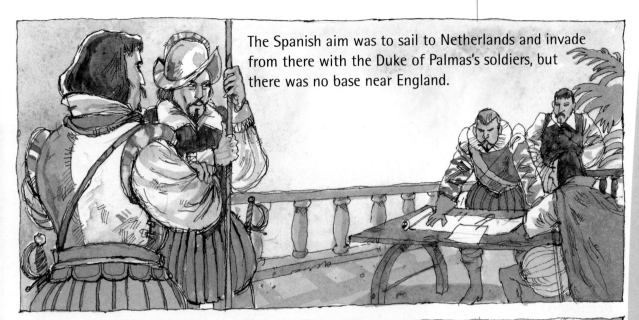

The Spanish aim was to sail to Netherlands and invade from there with the Duke of Palmas's soldiers, but there was no base near England.

Elizabeth makes a speech to her troops at Tilbury, while they are waiting to be attacked. She encourages them to be brave and increases their morale.

The Spanish fleet faced storms even as it tried to return home. Only 69 out of 140 ships got home safely.

EFFECTS OF THE ARMADA

England celebrated and Elizabeth took much of the credit. Following the humiliating defeat the Spanish threat to Elizabeth's rule died down. Although Philip continued to cause trouble for Elizabeth, he would not plan a direct invasion again. As the Spanish had not taken over England, Elizabeth was able to continue to help the Protestants in the Netherlands to fight against Philip. The Spanish built up their navy, determined never again to be defeated in such a way. This ended some of the raids of English sailors on Spanish ships.

SOURCE 1

The Armada portrait of Queen Elizabeth I, painted in 1588 to celebrate the defeat of the Spanish Armada.

Question Time

1. In pairs, make a list of all the reasons why the Armada failed. Try to write the most important reasons at the top of the list and the least important ones further down. Compare your lists with another couple. What do you notice?

2. Philip II's reaction to the Spanish defeat was 'I sent you out to war with men, not the wind and waves.'
   a What does Philip blame for the defeat of the Armada?
   b Do you agree that this is the main reason that they lost?
   c Are you surprised that Philip blames the weather rather than his men or the strength of the English fleet?

3. What message does the portrait in Source 1 on this page give us about Elizabeth and the Armada?

4. How did England gain from the Armada? Did they lose anything at all?

HOW DID ELIZABETH DEAL WITH THE PROBLEM OF MARRIAGE?

When we think of getting married, most of us think of finding a partner we love, someone with whom we would choose to spend the rest of our lives. For most Tudor women, especially wealthy ones, marriage was very different indeed. Rarely did people marry for love. The purpose of marriage was to produce heirs and so keep each family line alive. Money and land were often involved as part of marriage contracts, and couples rarely had a close relationship before their marriage, if at all.

The average age of marriage for women in this time was 20. So when Elizabeth came to the throne at the age of 24, she was expected to marry quite soon. How wrong people were!

WHY WAS MARRIAGE A PROBLEM FOR ELIZABETH?

Marriage for Elizabeth would not be easy. After all it would be no ordinary marriage. She had to think about the future of the country as well as that of her family and herself.

Here are some of the issues that Elizabeth had to think about:
- What religion should her husband follow? This could cause religious unrest in England. Most of the foreign princes were Catholic. She would be bound to upset one religious group or another.
- Should she marry a foreigner or someone from England, as Parliament preferred?
- Should she marry a member of a royal family or a nobleman?

SOURCE 1

A picture, painted in 1601, showing one of Elizabeth's progresses.

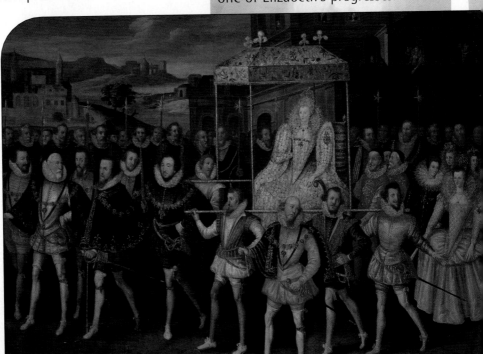

Parliament wanted Elizabeth to marry. Hopefully, this would bring England an heir. It thought that uncertainty over the future of the throne encouraged plotters and could lead to civil war when Elizabeth died. In 1562 Elizabeth nearly died from smallpox. Parliament began to panic. So why did Elizabeth delay – was she just fussy or indecisive, or were there other problems?

Elizabeth could also have been scared of marriage. After all many women in Tudor times died in childbirth. If she died with no safe heir what would happen to the country?

Marriage to one person would make others jealous. This could create enemies amongst foreign rulers or her own courtiers. She had learned from her cousin Mary's disastrous marriages that this could cause trouble.

She also liked to let foreign rulers and English nobles think that they might have a chance of marriage. It gave her power over them.

Tell my ministers that I am young enough to have many children...I just have no exact plans – yet...

Perhaps Elizabeth enjoyed her reputation as a virgin Queen. She used it to impress people and make her special.

SO WHO WERE THE MAIN CONTENDERS FOR THE JOB OF KING OF ENGLAND? HERE ARE FIVE OF THE MAIN SUITORS. WHO DO YOU THINK SHE SHOULD MARRY?

Philip of Spain

Approximately six years older than Elizabeth, he was a very strong Catholic and desperate to expand his power. He ruled over Spain, the Netherlands, Portugal and parts of South America. He had been married to Elizabeth's half-sister, Mary I, for four years before she died. He was one of the most powerful men in Europe.

Duke of Alençon

He was the youngest brother of the King of France. In 1579 he came to England on a secret visit to Elizabeth. He was short and pockmarked, but Elizabeth called him 'my frog' and liked his company although he was twenty years younger than her. He was unpopular in England as the French were famous for being anti-Protestant. France supported England in the war against the Spanish. He was a strong Catholic, but helped the Netherlands fight against the Spanish.

Earl of Leicester

His real name was Robert Dudley and he was Elizabeth's childhood friend; they were almost the same age. He was one of her favourites at court. He often escorted the queen on official duties. He lived at the wonderful Kenilworth Castle. Elizabeth had stayed there and been made very welcome with fine food and parties. He was good company and trusted by Elizabeth to be a link between her and her council. He had lost most of his fortune when imprisoned by Mary I and he spent more than he earned on clothes, the arts and good living. He showed his bravery fighting the French and was so popular with Elizabeth that he had enemies. He was also suspected of having affairs. His family were Protestant. He got married when he was 17 years old to Amy Robsart, who later died under mysterious circumstances.

Earl of Essex

His real name was Robert Devereux and he was the Earl of Leicester's stepson. He was a very handsome and strong-willed young man, 34 years younger than Elizabeth. He showed his courage fighting in the Netherlands and in France. He was popular with the people for his looks and dashing personality. He became wealthy from receiving the taxes from all sweet wines brought into the country.

William, Prince of Orange

He was also called William the Silent, and was almost the same age as Elizabeth. He was the Protestant leader of the rebellion against the Spanish in the Netherlands. He owned land in Germany, France and Holland.

Question Time

1 Why was Parliament so concerned that Elizabeth should have a safe heir to the throne as soon as possible?

2 'I am already bound to a husband, which is the Kingdom of England.' This was Elizabeth's reaction to Parliament when it again asked about her marriage plans. Why do you think that she gave this answer?

3 Fill in this chart to find out the strengths and weaknesses of each of Elizabeth's main suitors.

	Wealth and lands	Family and religion	Personality and looks	Popularity	Main strengths	Main problems
Philip II of Spain						
Duke of Alençon						
Earl of Leicester						
Earl of Essex						
Prince of Orange						

4 If Elizabeth was to ask each of these men to sum up in one sentence why she should marry them, what would each of them say?

5 You have had a look at each of the main suitors. It's advice time – who do you think Elizabeth should have married? Remember to think of implications for the country and not just Elizabeth. Give reasons why marriage to some of the other suitors would have been an unwise move to make.

WHY DID ALL THE MARRIAGE PROPOSALS FAIL?

Robert Dudley, Earl of Leicester, fell out of favour with Elizabeth by accepting the position of Governor General in the Netherlands. She did forgive him and he went on to take command of the English forces waiting for the arrival of the Spanish Armada. He stayed unpopular with the people of England and died in 1588.

The Duke of Alençon died in 1584, so marriage talks went no further.

Robert Devereux, the Earl of Essex, had 'pushed his luck' one time too many. He disobeyed Elizabeth many times and they had several public arguments. She usually forgave him, but when he failed on a mission in Ireland, he was banished from court. He tried to plot the overthrow of Lord Burghley. He was caught, tried for treason and executed at the age of 34.

William, Prince of Orange, was assassinated in 1584.

LEAVING IT TOO LATE

By the time the Armada was defeated, Elizabeth was 54 years old, far too old to have children and produce an heir. She had solved many of her problems as England was mostly a united and safe county. But one large problem still remained. What would happen to the throne of England after her death?

Question Time

Make a list of the benefits of not marrying and also the problems. Which list is longer? Do you think that Elizabeth should have married?

HOW DID ELIZABETH DEAL WITH THE PROBLEM OF POOR PEOPLE AND BEGGARS?

We often see on the news items about the problem of poverty in England. In Tudor times the problem of poor people was just as great and Elizabeth had to do something about it. Poor people in England today get help in many ways from the government and from various charities. Who could and should help in Elizabethan England? And who deserved to be helped anyway?

THE PROBLEM OF POVERTY

More and more people were becoming desperately poor in Elizabethan England. They no longer had the monasteries to give them help, and changes in the farming system closed off open common land that the poor could have used to graze their animals. A rise in sheep farming also meant that fewer workers were needed and so unemployment rose. When the prices of goods rose more than wages the poor got even poorer.

About 10,000 out of 5 million people were probably making their living by begging or stealing. In some families children were deliberately injured to get sympathy and more chance of help. Gangs of poor, fit and healthy people, found that stealing was easier than working or begging. Vagabonds took to the streets to look for work. Rich people were getting very worried about this problem. Law and order was being destroyed by the gangs roaming the towns and villages. But also many people believed that not working was lazy and sinful. Action had to be taken.

Lazy, fit beggar

Injure yourself or your child

Pretend to be mentally ill, for example by eating soap so that you frothed at the mouth

Pretend to have an injury like a leg missing

Steal washing from people's clothes lines to sell

SOURCE 1

An engraving from a sixteenth-century book showing the different types of beggars. As this engraving was printed at the time it shows that people were worried about beggars.

THE DIFFERENT TYPES OF POOR

Elizabeth's government decided to work out categories for different types of poor people. Some poor people were old, children, sick or infirm, and were genuine cases for help. They were called the 'deserving' poor. Others were able-bodied and so could be working, although they chose not to. These people were called the 'undeserving' poor.

ELIZABETH'S ACTION ON POVERTY

One of the main problems was to make sure that any money raised went to people who really deserved it. Henry VIII and Edward VI had already passed laws against beggars who were healthy and could get work. They were often whipped or branded as a punishment.

The problem of the poor was discussed in three of the thirteen sessions of Parliament during Elizabeth's reign. We know how many other problems she had, but her Parliament found time to pass laws. Elizabeth's ministers needed to raise money to deal with the problem. Her priority was to punish and deal with the dishonest poor and help the genuine cases.

SOURCE 2

The poor are divided into three sorts. Some are poor and cannot do anything to help themselves, like the fatherless child, the old, blind or lame, and the person with an incurable disease. The second are poor by accident, like the wounded soldier...The third sort are the poor who cannot save money, like rioters, vagabonds who wander from place to place and rogues who pretend to be ill.

William Harrison wrote this in 1587.

SOURCE 3

- *every parish would collect a poor rate (tax) to help the poor*
- *parishes could set up a House of Correction and force the able-bodied poor to work there.*
- *the poor had to stay in their own parish*
- *parishes would also look after the disabled poor and poor children.*

An extract from the 1601 Poor Law.

SOURCE 4

The churchwardens of every parish and four well-off house owners shall be called overseers of the poor. They shall set to work the children of all parents who shall not be thought able to keep and support their children, and also all persons, who married or unmarried, having no means to keep them, use no ordinary and daily trade of life to get their living by.

An extract from the Tudor Poor Law.

DID IT WORK? HISTORIANS DISAGREE ABOUT HOW SUCCESSFUL ELIZABETH'S POOR LAWS ACTUALLY WERE.

Here are some opinions by historians about Elizabeth's Poor Laws.

- They did nothing to stop the poor being poor, but saved some people from extreme starvation.

- The rich had to pay a lot more, the population increased and bad harvests meant that many were still starving.

- They did work out the difference between different types of poor so that they could help the really deserving people. Norwich, for example, cut the numbers of able-bodied poor by 90 per cent.

- They were still not really tackling why people were poor in the first place, but the system was an improvement which lasted for nearly 250 years.

Question Time

1 How does the government help poor people in England today?

2 What other help can poor people get in the twenty-first century?

3 The person in charge of giving out the poor relief in each parish was called the overseer. Would he have helped each of the characters below? Remember that they would have to be deserving poor to get money from the poor rate. The alternative might be punishment or the House of Correction.
  a Person 1 – woman with large family seen begging in local town with her children.
  b Person 2 – man whose leg had been mangled in an accident with a cart could not get a job.
  c Person 3 – man who had lost his job on a farm and wandered the county looking for work, sometimes disguised as a cripple.

4 Have you made the same decision as the rest of your class? Find some people who disagree with each other and find out why.

5 Which of the interpretations above, on this page, could be described as positive about Elizabeth's Poor Laws?

6 Which could be described as negative?

7 Which is the odd one out and why?

8 What do you and your class think about the success of Elizabeth's Poor Laws?

9 Do we have the same problems in dealing with the poor today?

DID ELIZABETH SUCCESSFULLY SOLVE THE PROBLEMS THAT BESET HER DURING HER REIGN?

Now it is time to come to some decisions about Elizabeth's reign. Was she a successful monarch? Historians disagree over this question. Some historians say that Elizabeth just avoided problems and was lucky rather than skilful.

Copy and fill in this chart to collect evidence from the work in this Unit.

Problem	Successful action	Problems that wouldn't go away	Marks out of 5 for overall success
Religious change			
Catholics and Puritans			
Competition for the throne – Mary, Queen of Scots			
The Spanish threat			
A husband			
Poverty in England			

Activity Time

1. In pairs, design a poster to show Elizabeth's problems, her solutions and how successful she was in dealing with each of them. Try to show which you think are the bigger problems for Elizabeth and which are the smaller ones. Use all the information from this Unit for ideas.

2. Compare your poster with the rest of the class. Are there any that have totally different ideas from yours? If so, why do you think that is?

3. As a class, decide on a final verdict for Elizabeth's reign. Then write some advice for her successor (whoever takes over from her). Use these sentences as a start if you like:

- When you start your reign you are lucky as you will not have to deal with...Elizabeth dealt with this when she...
- We think that you should watch out for the problem of.........because ....You could learn from Elizabeth because she.............................
- If you do as well as Elizabeth in the area of............you will be considered a successful monarch because.............
- If you have as many problems with........then the History books might not be a nice about you in the future. We think that you should........

Good Luck – you'll need it!

Unit 6: What were the achievements of the Islamic states 600–1600?

WHAT IS ISLAM?

About twenty per cent of the world population today are followers of the religion of Islam. In the Middle Ages, Islamic rulers created an empire in Arabia, which lasted for many centuries. This great empire spread to Palestine, North Africa, the Middle East and as far west as Spain. Between about 600 and 1000 this was the greatest civilisation in the world, and Islamic countries are very important in world affairs today. People in this empire were held together by similar beliefs, laws and customs. Many of them spoke Arabic. Before we can investigate the many achievements of the Islamic Empire we need to understand the key beliefs of Muslims (people who follow the religion of Islam) and how the religion was founded.

WHAT WAS PEOPLE'S RELIGION BEFORE ISLAM?

In the Middle East some people were Christian or Jewish. Many others worshipped many different gods or idols.

The five Pillars of Islam.

| To believe in one God whose messenger is Muhammad | To pray five times a day | To give to the poor | To fast during Ramadan | To make a pilgrimage, called the Hajj, to Mecca |

WHO FOUNDED ISLAM?

Muhammad was born in Mecca in Arabia in 570. He founded the religion of Islam and became a prophet (teacher who gives messages received from God). Muslims believe that Muhammad is the last and greatest of God's prophets.

WHAT HAPPENED AND WHEN?

In 610 AD, at the age of 40, Muslims believe Muhammad began to receive messages from God in the form of wonderful poems. He told other people these important messages. People began to listen to Muhammad's teaching and soon became Muslims. He was an honest man and became a highly respected leader. He advised people in every aspect of their lives.

WHAT HAPPENED TO ISLAM AFTER MUHAMMAD DIED?

Muhammad's teachings were written down in Arabic after he died and formed the Islamic Holy Book, called the Qur'an. Muslims also learn from Muhammad's example in a book called the Hadith, which includes examples from his life and many of his wise sayings.

Leaders called 'caliphs' took over after Muhammad. The word 'caliph' means 'deputy'. Some of these leaders argued with each other about how to rule and who should rule next. Arabic Muslim armies defended their religion and soon acquired a huge empire. Later, this empire was taken over by Turkish Muslims and eventually began to break up.

Activity Time

1 Create a glossary page to collect key words that you come across in this Unit. You could set it out like the chart below. Fill in your glossary for the three words/phrases given. Check your spelling carefully.

Islamic history – Key Word	What does it mean?
Qur'an	
Hadith	
Caliph	

2 We are going to use many different historical sources in our investigation of the Islamic states. Flick through the pages in this Unit and list six different types of evidence that we can use.

3 Can you think of two problems that we might have with historical evidence about the Islamic states between 600 and 1600?

4 Muslims get their ideas from the Qur'an and Hadith. They also follow the five Pillars of Islam which are their basic beliefs. Muslims believe that all aspects of their life should be influenced by Muhammad's teachings. All Islamic laws are based on these and cover everything from not eating pork or drinking alcohol to taxes, business and family life. Muslims also believe that Islam is the one true religion. Why do you think that these five basic rules are called **pillars**?

HOW DID THE WORLD OF THE MIDDLE EAST CHANGE DURING THE LIFE OF THE PROPHET MUHAMMAD AND THE FIRST FOUR CALIPHS?

EXPANSION DURING MUHAMMAD'S LIFETIME

Islam spread rapidly to take over Arabia in just 22 years. But Muhammad's teachings were not popular with everyone at first. The messages he said he received from God included ideas that criticised the way the old leaders ruled. This meant that Muhammad was unpopular in Mecca, his home town. He was chased out and moved to Medina in 622.

Success in Medina Muhammad became leader in Medina and as Islam became popular Medina became a state for Muslims. He ruled wisely and made treaties with other local tribes to keep the peace. Many of these tribesmen became Muslim too, and so increased the numbers. This meant that Islam became strong enough to fight against the Meccans. In 630 they beat them and gained Mecca for Islam.

Expansion Muslim ideas spread and armies took land from the other two main empires in the Middle East. These were Byzantium (the Eastern Roman Empire called the Byzantine Empire) and Persia (the Persian Empire).

WHAT HAPPENED AFTER THE DEATH OF MUHAMMAD?

The first four caliphs who ruled Muslim lands after Muhammad were his friends and relatives. They aimed to follow his ideas and example, and helped to spread Islam to new lands and quickly built a huge empire.

- First Caliph – Abu Bakr (632–4). Began to build Islamic Empire.
- Second Caliph – Umar (634–44) – murdered
- Third Caliph – Uthman (644–56) – murdered
- Fourth Caliph – Ali (656–61) – murdered

In 661, after the murder of Ali, there was a split between different groups of Muslims over who should rule next. This meant that there were many more assassinations and several different families (called dynasties) ruled. One leader no longer ruled over all the Muslim Empire.

Question Time

1. What are the advantages (good points) of having one main ruler in charge of a large empire like the Muslim one? Remember to explain your answer.

2. Can you think of any disadvantages (bad points) of having one main ruler in charge of a large empire?

WHERE WAS THE ISLAMIC EMPIRE?

The spread of the Islamic Empire during the sixth and seventh centuries.

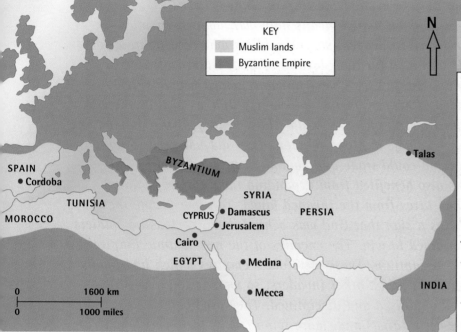

KEY
Muslim lands
Byzantine Empire

N

SPAIN
• Cordoba
BYZANTIUM
TUNISIA
MOROCCO
SYRIA
CYPRUS • Damascus
• Jerusalem
Cairo
EGYPT
• Medina
PERSIA
• Talas
INDIA
• Mecca

0 — 1600 km
0 — 1000 miles

Timeline of Islamic expansion

Islamic state in Medina.	**625**
Mecca successfully taken over by Medina Muslims.	**630**
The Muslim armies take over Jerusalem, Damascus and the whole of Syria. Persia fell next.	**640**
Cairo invaded and Egypt becomes Muslim.	**642**
Cyprus captured.	**649**
Tunisia and then Morocco become part of the Islamic Empire.	**670**
Muslim armies reach the western borders of India.	**707**
Cordoba in Spain taken.	**711**
Central Asia Muslim after the Battle of Talas.	**751**

Question Time

Q

1 On your own copy or a traced copy of this map plot the route of the spread of Islam. The different stages are on the timeline (right). Use arrows to show the direction of the spread of the empire. Work out how many kilometres the empire stretched from east to west and north to south.

2 Winning a battle like the Battle of Talas (see timeline) is only the start of an invasion. What else would the Muslim armies and leaders have to do to make an invaded land really 'Muslim'?

WHY WAS ISLAM SO SUCCESSFUL IN ITS EARLY YEARS?

Muslims believe that the main reason for the success of Islam is that it was what God wanted. As historians we need to investigate the other reasons to do with human actions and what happened. Read the box 'The Success of Islam' on page 162 to learn several different reasons why the Islamic Empire spread so fast and so easily in its early years.

Factfile: The Success of Islam

The Holy Qur'an included messages to spread Islam, so Muslims believed that it was their duty to expand the empire. They believed that they had a duty to carry out jihad, which means holy war, against enemies. Muslims also believed in heaven, so any soldiers who died fighting for Islam would be rewarded for their loyalty to God. Islam was a very attractive religion. Its laws were very fair and helped people's lives improve. The idea of heaven meant that poor people as well as the rich had hope. Tribes from all over the Middle East benefited from having one set of laws, one language and one religion. They did not need to fight with each other and could trade and communicate much more easily. Arabic Muslims also benefited from expanding their empire; gaining trade, wealth and taxes from the invaded lands. To some people these gains were seen as a sign that God was behind them, so Muslim soldiers were more determined to win. The enemies of the new Islamic Empire were Persia and Byzantium. These were older empires which had fought with each other and against other invaders, so were weaker. Muslim armies were well organised and disciplined. They used camels as transport in the desert areas and, more importantly, were very determined to win battles for God. Once lands had been invaded and added to the new empire, Muslims treated people with respect. They did not destroy buildings or ban other religions. This gained Islam more support and converts (people who became Muslims). Many conquered people even joined the Muslim army.

THE RULE OF THE CALIPHS

The first four Caliphs of Islam became known as 'Rightly Guided Caliphs' because they stuck closely to the teachings of Muhammad. They were seen as 'protectors' of Islam and were rulers, in charge of laws, army and religion. Unlike Muhammad, they were not considered prophets and did not claim to receive guidance from God. They had Muhammad's teachings and example to follow. They ruled wisely and soon expanded the Islamic Empire, gaining people's respect.

SOURCE 1

In the name of God, the Merciful, the Compassionate. Become Muslims and be saved. If not, accept our protection and pay taxes to us. Or else I shall come against you with men who love death as you love to drink wine.

Ibn Al Walid, a Muslim General, wrote this to the leaders of Persian tribes in 636.

Factfile: Caliph Umar

Caliph Umar was a friend of Muhammad's and ruled from 634-44. He was a huge man; some people say he was a giant. He was also a gentle person, although one account tells us that he had a bad temper. He stuck so closely to the example of Muhammad that he was given the title 'Commander of the Faithful'. He did not have many possessions and always wore very simple clothes. His decisions and laws were always fair. When he invaded Jerusalem in 638, he rode straight to the place where Muslims believe that Muhammad ascended to heaven. He asked to visit Christian churches, including the Church of the Holy Sepulchre. It is believed that this church is built around Jesus's tomb and is very special to Christians. During his visit there it was time for Muslim prayer. Umar could have prayed in the church, but he left out of respect for the Christians. He did not want his followers to turn it into a Muslim mosque. Umar let Christians and Jews have legal rights. They did not have to convert to Islam (become Muslims). The story also is told that Umar had travelled to Jerusalem on a camel which he had taken turns to ride with his servant. Umar did not, however, want total peace. He encouraged Muslims to fight to protect Islam and to win battles against any enemies.

Question Time

1 Define the word jihad and add it to your glossary.

2 Why would the idea of treating invaded areas and people with respect be a wise one? Explain your answer.

3 How many different reasons does Source 1 give us to explain Muslim success in taking over new lands?

4 Does Ibn Al Walid (Source 1) seem to be a wise or a foolish leader?

5 Find several different reasons for Islamic success in the 'Success of Islam' Factfile. Can you split up the different ideas? Create a cracker diagram like the one below to show why Islam was so successful. Copy the diagram and fill in each of the different reasons in the correct place.

Money from trade

A sign that God is alongside

Treated captured lands well

Strengths of Islam

Why was the spread of Islam so successful?

Weaknesses of enemies

Older and weaker empires

6 Were there any different causes which you found? Put them in the correct place or category. Some of these reasons are connected together. Draw arrows between any different reasons that you think are linked.

SOURCE 2

This peace guarantees them (Christians) security for their lives, their property, churches and the crucifixes (crosses). They shall not be forced to change their faith.

From the treaty signed by Umar.

Question Time

1 List five qualities that you think make a good leader. Which is most important?

2 You have been asked to give a talk to an historical conference. The talk is entitled 'Caliph Umar, a great ruler'.

a List the Caliph's strengths.

b Can you find any weaknesses? – if so list these, too.

c Choose three different strengths and explain them to show how each one makes him so successful. Remember that when you explain something you should use words or phrases like 'this means that...' and 'and so...' to help you.

d What is the one main thing that you think other leaders at the time have learnt from Umar? Explain your choice.

3 Do you think that the Islamic Empire would have spread so successfully if the first caliphs had been weak leaders?

WELCOME TO BAGHDAD – CENTRE OF THE ISLAMIC EMPIRE

If you were able to build a brand new capital city, what would you want to include in it? Would you want to have plenty of entertainment or housing or parks? Make a list of the features that would be on your planning list and share your ideas with the rest of the class.

Were your ideas similar to those of other people in your class? What do your choices tell us about life today and our priorities? What sort of things seem most important to us in the twenty-first century? We can use the planning and building of the ancient city of Baghdad to tell us all about Islamic priorities and way of life.

THE CITY OF BAGHDAD

The spectacular city of Baghdad was founded in 762 and became the centre of the Muslim Empire until 1258. It was built by the Abbasid dynasty (family) who were caliphs between 750 and 1055. They were the second dynasty to take over ruling after the 'Rightly Guided

Caliphs'. Remember that the caliphs would receive taxes from all over the empire and so became very wealthy. As a capital city that was sited on two rivers, Baghdad became a centre for traders and that brought in even more wealth. The traders also brought with them new ideas from all over the Islamic Empire and from China, Africa and Russia.

BUILDING BAGHDAD

The caliph who organised the building of Baghdad was al-Mansur (754-775). Baghdad was the second-largest city in the world at that time, with 1.5 million people. 100,000 men worked to build it over four years before the Caliph could move in. It contained over 1000 mosques and 65,000 public baths, and had sewers and clean water fountains, as well as a complex irrigation system that took water from the Rivers Tigris to make the soil fertile. Houses, palaces, markets, shops, gardens, hospitals, race tracks and a paper factory were all added in the 100 years after it was founded, with a 'House of Wisdom' set up in the ninth century. Caliph Harun al Rashid became fabulously rich and expanded Baghdad even further between 786 and 809.

SOURCE 1

Baghdad was built in the form of a huge circle nearly two miles across with a deep moat surrounding three huge sloping walls. Of these, the middle one was the largest, some 112 feet in height, 164 feet wide at the base and 46 feet wide across the top. It was fortified with look-out towers. The round city was cut into four wedge-shaped parts by two highways which cut across it at right angles, with gates through each of the walls. The space between the middle and outer walls was left clear for defence. Between the middle and outer walls were the houses of the courtiers and army officers. Behind the inner walls lived the caliph's relatives and the most important officials. The hub of the city was the caliph's palace. Between the inner and middle walls each of the main streets became lined with all manner of shops, making four central markets. The ordinary people of Baghdad lived outside the walls.

From a history book about Early Islam, written in the 1960s.

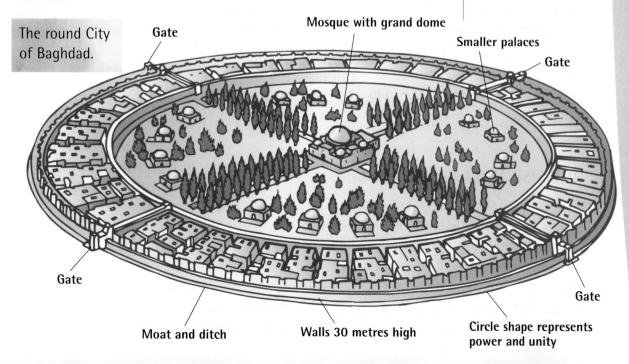

The round City of Baghdad.

Gate

Mosque with grand dome

Smaller palaces

Gate

Gate

Moat and ditch

Walls 30 metres high

Circle shape represents power and unity

Gate

Question Time

1. Make a copy of the drawing of Baghdad on page 165. Add further labels to it using the information that is given in Source 1.

2. Which do you think would be more useful to an historian studying Baghdad at this time, Source 1 or the drawing?

3. What can we find out about the caliphs of early Baghdad by looking at its layout and buildings? Prepare a short presentation of your findings to give to the rest of the class. Include the following ideas about the caliphs of Baghdad: their importance, their priorities, wealth, protection, and also how they could be criticised.

4. What sort of things don't these sources tell us?

DAILY LIFE IN EARLY BAGHDAD

Ancient Baghdad contained 1.5 million people at its time of greatest power. In addition to this population many traders visited Baghdad, selling their products or buying goods to take to other parts of the empire. What was it like to live in Baghdad?

THE RISE AND FALL OF BAGHDAD

Baghdad was the centre of the early empire but slowly the power of the caliphs declined. They began to be influenced by military leaders and soldiers who told them how to rule. This marked the end of the early way of ruling.

Factfile: Baghdad

Trade

Trade was the main purpose of this wonderful city. The caliph employed his own officer to buy and sell goods and so he grew very rich on the profits. The caliph also charged the traders tolls and rents. The traders themselves came from as far as China, Russia and Spain. There were many different markets, called souks, in Baghdad, selling everything from pottery and leather goods to flowers and food. All markets had strict rules to keep trade fair. Inspectors visited stalls to check on the quality and quantity of goods sold. Poor quality produce meant that a trader could be fined. People were scared that the caliph's officials would punish them strictly.

Arts, Education and Health

The caliphs wanted their capital city to represent the whole Empire. They wanted to show off their wealth, their power and their talent. They decorated houses and palaces with beautiful mosaics and tiles. The Qur'an also encouraged education, so there were libraries to

Food and Entertainment

The variety of food available in Baghdad was huge. But the range and quality of meals eaten would depend upon whether you were rich or poor. For the rich there was fish, chicken or lamb, with delicious sauces made from different nuts, herbs and milk. Many meals turned into feasts with up to 40 different dishes. One special sweet was sherbet which was very popular. The poor ate rice bread and cheap meat. Women and children ate separately from the men.

A trip to the races was a good way to relax after a busy day at the market. Men would also play chess, polo and archery. Remember that the city also had many parks and open spaces, although the noise and smells from the crowded city would be very noticeable.

Other Work

There were many other jobs in Baghdad besides that of a merchant or trader. These included shopkeepers, dock workers, weavers, builders and keepers of mosques. Rich people often had slaves to work for them. The slaves were not Muslims, but often prisoners of war. They had to be treated well and cared for. The caliph himself employed many people as guards, police, soldiers, officials and servants.

Officials of the caliph dressed in long black robes so they stood out in a busy street. They would watch out for anyone disobeying the caliph's rules.

visit. One caliph even built a special House of Wisdom, an early university. Mosques also kept collections of books for people to study.

If you were unwell you could visit one of the many doctors who would examine and treat you for a small fee. People washed regularly and kept themselves clean for Allah (God). This meant that there were many public baths and fountains with clean water in the city.

SOURCE 2

Near the mosque you will find the souk of the bookseller, the souk of the bookbinders, and as its neighbour, the souk of the leather merchants and the market of slippers. Approaching the gates of the town one will find the makers of saddles and those pack saddles whose customers are country people. Then the food sellers together with the basket makers. At the edge of the town because they require space and because they are thought undesirable: the dyers, the tanners, and almost outside the city limits, the potters.

Ibn Bututa, a traveller, describes the separate markets of Baghdad.

SOURCE 4

They are numerous and well made. Each establishment has a number of private bathrooms. Every one has a wash basin in the corner, with two taps supplying hot and cold water.

Every bather is given three towels, one to wear around his waist when he comes out, and two to dry himself. In no other town than Baghdad have I seen these arrangements.

Ibn Bututa describes Baghdad's public baths.

SOURCE 3

This manuscript illustration from the twelfth century shows wealthy citizens enjoying entertainment in a garden in Baghdad.

SOURCE 5

A picture of the Mongol siege of Baghdad in 1258, drawn in Persia in the fifteenth century.

The army had more power than the caliphs who took orders.	*850*
Persian Buyids took over ruling Baghdad, but the army still told them what to do.	*945*
Turkish Muslims, called the Seljuk Turks, invaded. Their leader became ruler, called a Sultan. The caliphs still had to take orders from someone else.	*1055*
Mongols sack (destroy) the city in a siege that lasted six days. The last Abbasid caliph is murdered and the Abbasid dynasty is finally over. Islamic lands are no longer one united empire and the caliphs no longer rule.	*1258*

Question Time

1 Why do you think that the caliph made his officials wear long black robes?

2 Can you think of two reasons why different goods were all sold in different markets in Baghdad?

3 Does Source 2 tell us which market goods were thought to be most valuable in early Baghdad? Explain your answer with evidence from the source.

4 The Mongols deliberately destroyed the irrigation system and most of the main buildings when they invaded Baghdad. Do you think this was a clever thing to do? Explain your answer.

5 Look carefully at Source 5.
   a Make a list of what you can see inside and outside the walls.
   b What is there in the source that makes you believe that it could be a realistic picture of Baghdad being attacked?
   c Is there enough evidence in the picture to convince you that it is Baghdad?
   d Why do you think the capture of Baghdad was such an important victory for Mongol invaders?

Activity Time

You have been asked to design a booklet showing people the splendour of Baghdad in the eleventh century. In your booklet you must include:

a the layout of the city

b trading places and business rules

c important sights and sounds

d what to be careful of and watch out for

e the caliph and his officers

f food, accommodation business rules and entertainment

g what he will be most impressed with and why

h any other important information for visitors

ISLAMIC THINKING – MATHS AND SCIENCE

Look at the words in the box below. You may need a dictionary to help you find the meaning of these words.

coffee	sherbet	orange	cheque	camel	alcohol
chemistry	average	zero	sodium	alkali	algebra

The Islamic religion encouraged learning. Famous books by Greek and Roman thinkers, such as Aristotle, were translated from Greek and Latin into Arabic. They were studied in the universities and libraries that existed in most Islamic towns. As a result of this enthusiasm to learn, many Muslims came up with new ideas or discoveries. They also developed old ideas further and helped to make great progress in the areas of maths and science.

SOURCE 1

- *Seek knowledge, even as far as China.*

- *The ink of the scholar is more sacred than the blood of the martyr.*

Two sayings of Muhammad about learning.

PROGRESS IN MATHS

The decimal system of counting is based on the Arabic changes to an old Hindu method. It makes arithmetic much easier and more logical and therefore is the basis for all mathematics, including calculations and algebra. Muslims also developed new theories in algebra and geometry. Muslims used their mathematical skill in practical situations, for example daily worship, farming, trade, building and architecture.

PROGRESS IN SCIENCE

Progress in science included the areas of medicine, alchemy, astronomy and astrology. Muslim thinkers were interested in observing the world around them. In particular, they studied the planets and the stars. They developed a Greek tool used for measuring their distance to stars and planets, the astrolabe. This equipment was used by travellers to tell the position of the stars. Muslim caliphs believed that the study of science, and medicine in particular, would help their health and so encouraged translations of the works of ancient doctors, such as Galen. Developments in science also helped progress in technology and other areas. For example, Muslim scientists developed magnifying lenses in the eleventh century.

Question Time

1 What do some of the words in the box on page 170 have in common?
   a Can you divide these words into three main groups? Explain your decision.
   b Can you see which two words seem to be the odd ones out?
   c What other categories could you split these words into?

2 Write out three hypotheses or conclusions about the words, for example one hypothesis would be 'The Arabs were interested in maths'. You should be able to say how far this conclusion is true by the end of this section.

3 How could advanced understanding of mathematics be used in three following areas: worship, farming, trade, building and architecture?

Arabic numbers

Helped to make calculations easier.

Alchemy

Science of how chemicals work, for example which ones can be used to make dyes and glazes.

Astrolabe

Helped to tell the time and travellers could work out their direction. Used to find the direction of Mecca and times for daily prayers too.

Question Time

1 How would the development of a magnifying lens help to make progress in medicine, and in science generally?

2 Using Source 1 on page 170 and any other information that you can find, explain how Islam encouraged progress in maths and science.

3 Your job is to teach the teachers a little more about Islamic maths and science! Produce a booklet that teachers could use in maths and science lessons to show students like you some of the history of their subjects. You should include several different Islamic discoveries and why they were important. Research a few more Islamic ideas about maths or science using some of the key words on page 170. Explain the contribution of each discovery. Remember that pictures and diagrams would make the teachers and the students more interested in what you have to say.

WHAT CAN WE LEARN FROM THE ARCHITECTURE OF ISLAMIC CIVILISATIONS?

The word for the design of buildings is architecture. Islamic architecture has become famous all over the world for its amazing detailed designs. The beauty of places like the Taj Mahal in India, Córdoba and the Alhambra Palace in Spain mean that they are admired around the world. When the Europeans were building motte and bailey castles from wood and stone, the Muslims were planning complex and beautifully decorated palaces and mosques.

Most mosques have similar features, connected to the purpose of the building and the religious beliefs of the Muslims who worship there. Compare the two medieval mosques in Sources 2 and 3 – one is in Spain, the other in Turkey, but they are similar. Mosques in our towns and cities today also have most of these features.

SOURCE 2

The interior of the mosque at Córdoba.

SOURCE 3

A photograph of the exterior of the mosque at Edirne.

SOURCE 4

Arabesque is the term used to describe the pattern of flowing lines with flowers and leaves. What does this word tell us about the Arabs?

Look closely at Sources 2 and 3. Then look at the key. Most mosques have the features in this key. You have probably already studied some of these in your Religious Education lessons.

Islamic art is based on geometric shapes and calligraphy, rather than paintings of people and animals. This is because Islamic teachers have said that as God is the only creator, man should not make images of living things.

KEY	
Minaret	tower from where the people are called to prayer
Dome	to represent the power of heaven over earth
Courtyard	mainly in hot countries
Fountain	for people to wash themselves for God before praying
Decoration	decorated arches with detailed carvings, geometric shapes and calligraphy (writing used as decoration)

Question Time

❶ Make a list of which features you can see in Sources 2 and 3.

❷ Describe to a friend what you see in Source 4. What do you notice about these examples of Islamic art?

A PALACE FIT FOR A KING

When the Muslims invaded most of Spain in 711 they brought their beliefs and their culture with them. Spain was ruled by the Umayyad caliphs even when they had been overthrown in the Middle East. Spain split into kingdoms and Islamic control was largely lost by 1212. The Muslims were finally chased out of Spain by the Christians by the end of the fifteenth century. Source 2 is the famous mosque in Córdoba in Spain. Córdoba was the capital of Muslim Spain. Sources 5 and 6 show parts of the Alhambra Palace in Granada in Spain. It took over 100 years to complete and contains many courtyards, fountains and magnificently decorated arches.

SOURCE 5

A modern photograph of the Alhambra Palace in Spain showing its strong walls and towers.

SOURCE 6

A modern photograph of the Alhambra Palace in Spain showing the beautiful fountains and gardens.

Question Time

1 What can Islamic buildings tell us about the Muslims who planned and built them? Use all the sources and information to answer this question. Mention:

a the different parts of the mosques
b the types of decoration used
c where the buildings are found
d the life of the people who lived in/visited them
e the skills and wealth needed to build them
f what image the patrons (people who paid for the buildings) wanted to create.

2 Now read back through your answer and look for two types of sentence:

a ones which we know are fact – based on our study so far
b ones which we think are true but are more like guesswork at this stage.
Underline all the **a** sentences in one colour and all the **b** sentences in another. Write a key to say which colour is **a** and which is **b**.

HOW SUCCESSFUL WERE THE CRUSADER ATTACKS AGAINST THE ISLAMIC WORLD?

The headline suggests that Jerusalem is in the headlines today, much as it was in the Middle Ages. It is a city that was and is still fought over. But why?

Peace talks in Middle East hit crisis – what is the future of Jerusalem? 9/4/99

JERUSALEM THE HOLY CITY

Jerusalem is a Holy City for Jews, Christians and Muslims. It contains the Wailing or Western Wall, the remaining wall of part of Herod's temple, a site of pilgrimage and prayer for Jews, the Church of the Holy Sepulchre, supposedly built on the site of Jesus' tomb, and Dome of the Rock mosque where Muhammad is said to have ascended to heaven. Many pilgrims visited Jerusalem and its holy places in the past, and still do today. When Muslim Caliph Umar took over Jerusalem in 638, he allowed the Christians and Jews freedom to worship, but in 1009 the Caliph of Egypt destroyed the Church of the Holy Sepulchre and Christians and Jews were no longer free. When the Seljuk Turks took over the empire, religious freedom was possible, but not definitely granted. It was still dangerous for pilgrims to visit Jerusalem.

THE CRUSADES

The Crusades were holy wars or 'invasions' of the land around Jerusalem. The Crusaders fought for 'the cross', or Christianity, which is why they are called 'Crusaders'. They were Christians who wanted to capture the 'Holy Land' from the Muslims. All sorts of people went on Crusades. Some people went to gain a fortune or for adventure, as well as for religious reasons. Whatever their motives (reasons), the Crusaders were prepared to face hardship and many problems on the journey from Europe which was over 3000 kilometres. Those who stayed at home paid high taxes or mortgaged out their land to pay for these wars. And what has Jerusalem got to do with the Crusades? Before we can answer the main question in this section we need to answer several others. Can you think of five different smaller questions that you will need to have answered even before you can answer this big question? Here are some to start with: What were the Crusades? Who were the Crusaders? Where did they come from? Why did they attack? What did they want? What did the Crusaders do? What happened to the Muslims? What was and still is so important about who rules Jerusalem?

See how many of these smaller questions are answered below.

THE BYZANTINE EMPEROR AND THE POPE

When Alexius, the Byzantine Emperor, asked Pope Urban II in 1095 to send men to help him to defeat the Muslims, many people all over Europe answered the Pope's request. They decided that enough was enough and wanted to take control of Jerusalem and the Holy Land for themselves. This would mean defeating the Muslims and making sure that Islamic laws and traditions were removed as well.

Activity Time

Make a list of the little questions that have not yet been answered, plus any more that you can think of. Carry out some research on the Crusades to try to find out a little more.

WHAT HAPPENED?

Thousands of people travelled to the Middle East. They fought against the Saracens, the Crusader name for the Muslims. Some of the Christians won land and settled there, some were defeated and returned home; others were killed. Christian kingdoms of Antioch, Edessa, Jerusalem and Tripoli were set up and some lasted for nearly 200 years.

THE BIG QUESTION

So, how successful were the Crusader attacks against the Islamic world? The word how in the title means that we need to try to work out whether the attacks were very/quite/not very/not at all successful. How can we measure the success of the crusades? Make a list of three different things that we could look at in order to decide how successful the Crusader attacks actually were. One example could be the amount of land captured by the Christians.

OVERVIEW OF THE CRUSADES

There were at least seven different crusades according to some historians. They spanned almost 200 years. In the first 50 years, the Christians gained a lot of land but over time the Muslim armies proved too strong for them. The Crusades meant that, although enemies, Christians and Muslims from Western Europe and the Middle East came into contact with each other. Although the Crusades lasted for many years, the fighting was not constant. There were long periods of peace where Christians and Muslims lived and worked together. Ideas were swapped. This is one reason why so many Islamic and Arabic influences are part of European cultures. Four different events, spread over 200 years, can show us how far the Muslims were seriously threatened by the Christians.

KEY EVENTS IN THE CRUSADES

1099 – The capture of Jerusalem This was the focus of the one of the first properly organised crusades and by far the most successful. Many Muslim leaders were busy fighting between themselves and were taken by surprise by this attack. However, it still took over a month to get through the strong walls into the city of Jerusalem. The Crusaders had little water and few supplies. They were also short of materials and weapons with which to attack. Just in time supply ships arrived and some wood was found ready to make tall siege towers, like the one in Source 2. The Crusaders captured Jerusalem for Christianity but celebrated by murdering many people – Muslims, Jews and Christians. Approximately 70,000 men, women and children were killed.

SOURCE 2

A picture from a fourteenth-century French manuscript showing Crusaders attacking the walls of Jerusalem.

SOURCE 1

A siege machine throwing heads into the town of Nicea.

Question Time

1. How would the siege machine shown in the front of Source 2 help the Crusaders to break through the city walls?

2. What other weapons can you see in this source?

3. Traditional weapons were not always successful against such strong walls in towns and fortresses. Why do you think that the Crusaders in Source 1 are hurling severed (chopped off) heads over the walls?

4. What impact would the events following the capture of Jerusalem have had on the Crusaders' reputation?

1187 – The Battle of Hattin Crusaders' attacks were not always successful and the Muslims had begun to win back land. Salah al-Deen (Saladin), the famous Turkish sultan and leader of the Muslims, beat the Crusaders. He took over the town of Tiberias and the Crusaders went to nearby Hattin to try to get it back. The Muslim army was huge and Salah al-Deen's tactic of attacking the Crusaders as they marched successfully weakened the men so that when the battle started the Muslims won easily. After this battle, he ordered all the Christian knights to be killed. Having wiped out the Crusader army, he was soon able to take over the Holy City of Jerusalem, capture the King of Jerusalem and take several other Crusader towns. When he captured Jerusalem, he did not murder any of the Christians inside. He either took ransom money to release them or sold them to become slaves.

1198 – The Fourth Crusade Salah al-Deen's capture of Jerusalem led to a Third Crusade led by Richard I of England. Although Richard won back Acre and Jaffa, the important city of Jerusalem stayed under Muslim control. This meant that a Fourth Crusade was needed. However this Crusade turned out to fight against the Greeks and actually captured Constantinople. This was the centre of the Eastern Christian Empire (Byzantine) but had been taken over by another group of Greek Christians. The Crusaders helped to remove them, but took the city for themselves rather than hand it back to the old emperor's family. So the Fourth Crusade was actually fought against other Christians! As a result Crusaders damaged their reputation and were seen to be a selfish army rather than one that was on a religious mission. The Muslims continued to win back land from the Crusaders in the Holy Land.

Question Time

❶ The Muslims were used to the climate in the Holy Land. How might this be an advantage to them and a disadvantage to the Crusaders?

❷ Why do you think that Salah al-Deen executed all the Crusader knights after the Battle of Hattin but did not kill the Christians in Jerusalem?

❸ Salah al-Deen was actually criticised for not killing more Christians after the Battle of Hattin. Why do you think this was?

❹ Research to find out why the Fourth Crusade was fought against the Christians rather than the Muslims.

❺ The artist's sketch on page 179 shows what happened to the city of Constantinople during the Fourth Crusade. How useful is this drawing to historians?

An artist's reconstruction of the seige of Constantinople.

SOURCE 3

The little Frankish (Crusader) states were now on their last legs. They were difficult to reinforce because Jerusalem was no longer in Christian hands, so there wasn't the supply of good class able bodied pilgrims who could be pressed into staying for a while and fighting. At the same time the standard of living rose and people were better off staying where they were.

An explanation of the reason for the end of Christian rule in the Holy Land, from a recent school book.

Question Time

❶ What reasons does Source 3 give for the eventual decline in Crusader strength in the Holy Land?

❷ Several different words are used to describe victories and defeats in battles. In 1291 the 'fall' of Acre took place. Does the word 'fall' suggest whether this event was good or bad? Who might have used this term, Muslims or Christians? Explain your answer carefully.

1291 – The fall of Acre Although the Christians owned only a few small states by 1250, the Muslims had split amongst themselves and so were not fighting back in any organised way. When only Acre and Tripoli remained Christian, the Muslims started to attack again. Acre was the very last town held by the Christians, who had ruled there for a 100 years. The Muslims outnumbered the Christians by five to one so did not take long to capture Acre. This symbolised the end of the Christian rule in the Holy Land. But Crusaders did carry on going on crusades to other areas – Spain and Prussia, for example.

Activity Time

A

❶ You are going to produce a timeline with a difference. It will actually include two different timelines in one. Look back at pages 177–9 and fill in on the flagpole the four main events that we have investigated so far. For each event show whether it was a victory for the Muslims or the Christians. Some events could have benefits for both groups.

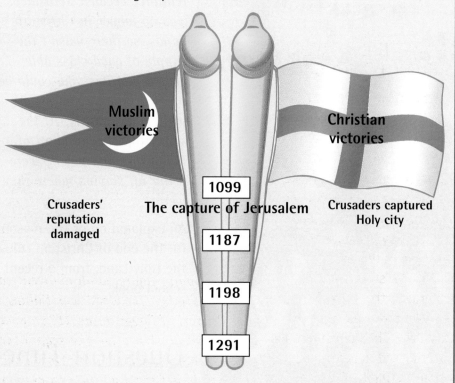

Muslim victories

Christian victories

Crusaders' reputation damaged

The capture of Jerusalem

Crusaders captured Holy city

1099

1187

1198

1291

❷ Research two more key events of the Crusades and add them to your timeline. Remember to show who gained the victory in each example.

❸ How successful would you say that the Crusader attacks actually were? Try to decide whether they were *very/quite/not very/not at all* successful and back up your ideas with proof from your timeline.

Use sentences like these to help:

- The Crusader attacks were successful in some ways because.....(give examples and reasons)

- However, they were also unsuccessful because..........

- Overall I think that.............

WHY DO PEOPLE DISAGREE ABOUT SALAH AL-DEEN?

This is a story of a warrior. He was brave, clever, cunning, determined, a man of honour but sometimes cruel. He was a Muslim leader from Egypt and helped to wipe out the Crusades in the Holy Land, but he was also admired in the West. Was he really a magnificent military leader or was he a tyrant? Historians disagree, so see what you think.

SALAH AL-DEEN AND THE BATTLE OF HATTIN AND CAPTURE OF JERUSALEM

His most famous battle is the Battle of Hattin (see page 178). Here his clever tactics paid off. He attacked the Crusaders as they were marching, when they were very short of water in the hot desert. This meant that when they came to fight in battle they were exhausted and were easily beaten. He was then able to wipe out the Christian army and take back Jerusalem (page 178). After this battle he famously executed the Christian army. Some people say this was cruel, others that it was a wise move to make. When he had captured Jerusalem, he allowed the Christians there to live. Some Muslims criticised him for this, other people say this was an example of how he was fair and did not really enjoy killing.

When the Crusaders came back on the Third Crusade, Salah al-Deen defended Jerusalem so well that Richard I of England and his army were prevented from regaining Jerusalem.

Who was Salah al-Deen?

A popular figure Salah al-Deen (called Saladin by Crusaders) was Sultan (leader) of Egypt. From 1176 onwards he led Muslim armies to regain their lost lands, including the Holy Land. Salah al-Deen's military campaigns helped to push out the Christians from the Middle East. Salah al-Deen fought against rival Muslim groups, too. He captured all of Egypt and Syria.

FAMOUS IN EAST AND WEST

Salah al-Deen was not just famous in the Middle East. Christians in England at the time were asked by King Richard I to pay a tax to fund the Third Crusade. They called this tax the Saladin Tithe (10 per cent tax on goods and money). Salah al-Deen had respected the determination of the Crusaders, but thought that they would have to be wiped out. He died of yellow fever in 1193, a hundred years before the final Muslim victory in the Crusades, but he was very important in regaining Muslim control of the area.

Question Time

1. Write the word Sultan and its meaning in your glossary.

2. English Christians named a tax after Salah al-Deen. Does this prove that he was unpopular in the West?

3. Why do you think that he is so important in the history of the Crusades? Below are three possible suggestions. Do you agree with any of them?

   a He is important because he killed lots of people.

   b He is important because his battles against the Crusaders were a turning point which left the Muslims in control of an area that had been fought over for over a hundred years.

   c He is important because he represents the Muslim victories.

4. Can you think of any other reasons why he is so important?

WHAT DID PEOPLE AT THE TIME THINK OF SALAH AL-DEEN?

SOURCE 1

To cut a long story short, so many were killed, so many made prisoner that even the enemy felt sorry for our people. Some of the prisoners were kept safe until Salah al-Deen had decided what to do with them. The rest were sent to heaven in a quick and merciful death by the murderous sword. Among the prisoners was Reynald of Chatillon. The tyrant (Salah al-Deen) cut off his proud head with his own hands. This was either because he was in a rage, or possibly out of respect for so great a man. All the Templars (fighting monks) who were captured, he ordered to be beheaded. He was determined to wipe them out, for he knew that they were stronger than him in battle.

After the Battle of Hattin, from a book about King Richard (*Itinerarium Regis Ricardi*) – by an English monk, 1200.

SOURCE 2

God – may he be honoured and glorified – gave the upper hand to the Sultan Salah al-Deen. God made straight for the Sultan the road leading to his enemies' destruction. If his only achievement was this one victory then he would still be above all the kings of former times let alone those of his age.

Salah al-Deen's victory at Hattin, from *The Book of Two Gardens* by Imad ad Din Al Isfahahani, Salah al-Deen's secretary.

SOURCE 3

A painting from an illuminated manuscript
showing Salah al-Deen taking the Holy Cross.

SOURCE 4

*I never saw him find the
enemy too powerful. He
would think carefully
about each aspect of the
situation and take the
necessary steps to deal
with it, without
becoming angry. At the
Battle of Acre, the centre
of the Muslim army was
broken, but he stood
firm with a handful of
men and led them into
battle again.*

Salah al-Deen's military
skill as described by his
official Baha al-Din.

Question Time

Study Sources 1-4 and then answer these
questions:

1 Why did Salah al-Deen kill Reynald,
according to Source 1?

2 Find two pieces of evidence in Source 1
that suggest that the monk who wrote
this source did not like Salah al-Deen.

3 Are you surprised that he seems biased?
Explain your answer giving more than
one reason if you can. A clue is to look
at who he was and the title of his book.

4 Are you surprised that Source 2 says
what it does about the sultan?

5 Source 3 shows Salah al-Deen winning
the Holy Cross (Christians believed that
this was part of the cross that Jesus was
crucified on). Does this suggest that he
was a good military leader?

6 Would you expect the author of Source
4 to tell the truth about Salah al-Deen?

7 Fill in this chart to sum up what people
at the time thought of Salah al-Deen.

Source	Written by Muslim or Christian?	Salah al-Deen shown as positive or negative? Give some proof.

8 What are your conclusions about Salah
al-Deen's reputation?

WHAT DO PEOPLE LATER IN HISTORY THINK OF SALAH AL-DEEN?

SOURCE 5

Salah al-Deen was a great warrior, but he was not rough and unmannerly. In fact the Arabs had strict rules about the treatment of guests. Even among people with such standards of good manners, Salah al-Deen stood out for his courtesy. To the Arabs, the Crusaders must have seemed rough and barbarous.

From *Pilgrimages and Crusades* by G Evans (1976).

SOURCE 6

In the nineteenth century the German Kaiser (Emperor) built a decorated marble tomb for Salah al-Deen at the place where he is buried. This was to celebrate his life.

This account shows that Salah al-Deen was considered a hero, even 700 years after his death.

SOURCE 7

A painting of Salah al-Deen with Saddam Hussein, the President of Iraq.

Question Time

Study Sources 5–7 and then answer the questions below.

1 Fill in this chart to find out what these sources say about Salah al-Deen.

Source	Who was it written by?	Salah al-Deen as positive or negative? (give evidence)

2 Compare your chart with the earlier one completed. What are your conclusions?

3 Can you suggest any reasons why Salah al-Deen's reputation seems to have changed over the centuries? Here are some suggestions – which do you think are most likely reasons?

  a New evidence has been found which proves that Salah al-Deen was a good man and never cruel.

  b Christians at the time realised that he had beaten them and so could not see his good qualities.

  c His battles are exciting stories of bravery and success which make him famous in any time period.

  d In the twenty-first century people can see that the Muslim culture was more advanced than the Christian one at the time of Salah al-Deen. This makes people think that Salah al-Deen was probably a very skilled and well-mannered man.

4 What more do you need to know about Salah al-Deen before you can come to a final conclusion about him?

5 Has your opinion of Salah al-Deen changed since the start of this section? Explain your answer.

RULING THE OTTOMAN EMPIRE

ENTER THE OTTOMANS

The Ottomans were Muslims from Turkey who took over many of the Islamic states in about 1400. Remember that the Islamic Empire had begun to break up after the rule of the caliphs and different parts were led by different Muslim rulers. They were also invaded by the Mongols. The Ottomans took over, then expanded their rule, invading European lands so that they eventually surrounded and swallowed up the old Byzantine Empire. The Ottoman Empire lasted until as late as 1924. It is named after the first Turkish leader to expand their control. He was called Osman.

This map charts the growth of the Ottoman Empire between the fourteenth and seventeenth centuries.

N

HOW DID THEY BECOME (AND STAY) SO POWERFUL? - THE OTTOMAN RECIPE FOR SUCCESS

Ingredient No. 1 – One famous capital city. By 1451, the Ottoman ruler Sultan Mehmet II wanted to take over Constantinople, which had always been a Christian city. It had been the centre of the Byzantine Empire (Eastern Roman Empire) until it was attacked in the Fourth Crusade (see page 178). It was a fine city and still a vital trading place. Its position acted almost as an entrance to the Ottoman Empire.

It took a six-week siege to take over the city, which was defended by 8000 men. Mehmet renamed it Istanbul, carried out a huge building plan and made the city the capital of his Ottoman Empire.

Ingredient No. 2 – A fine fighting force. Instead of raising taxes and having to pay men to join his army, the Ottoman Sultan came up with a good idea. Young Christian boys from the area were captured and trained as special highly skilled soldiers, easily recognisable by their white headgear. They had to become Muslims. They were devoted to the sultan and the army for life. The Ottomans also developed a fine navy and advanced weapons. They even paid pirates from North Africa to fight for them. As a result, the Ottomans were feared all over the Middle East and southern Europe.

Ingredient No. 3 – Magnificent wealth and beautiful buildings. Mehmet would not let the magnificent Byzantine buildings be destroyed and he built many more fine palaces, mosques, schools, baths and hospitals. The sultan's main palace kitchens were so big that they employed over a thousand people. Istanbul became the most wonderful city in the Muslim world. The Ottoman sultans became admired and respected.

0   160

0   1000

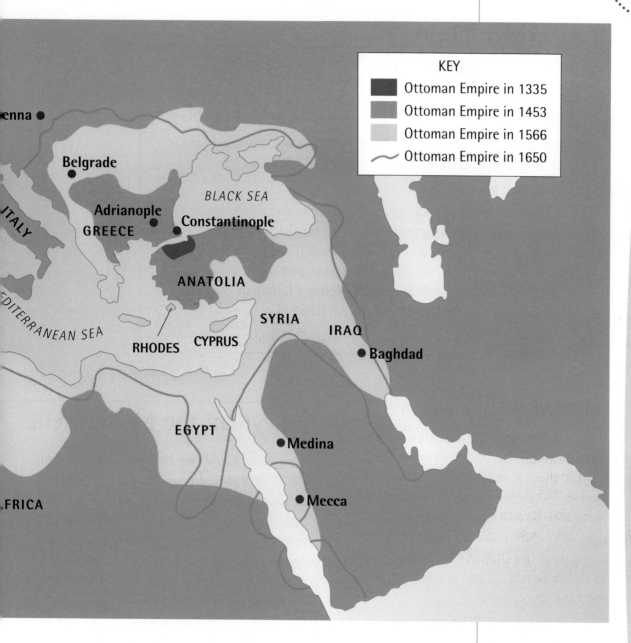

Ingredient No. 4 – Strict laws all over the Empire. The sultans not only kept people under tight control in their palaces and main cities. They had judges called qadis who had studied Islamic laws and these judges used the examples in the Qur'an to advise them in their decisions. Punishments were severe. You could have your hand chopped for stealing, for example. People believed that these punishments were fair and would keep order in the empire.

SOURCE 1

Mehmet himself chose the best place in the middle of the city and ordered a mosque to be built there which would rival the biggest and finest for height, beauty and size.

Kritovoulus, Mehmet II's biographer, describing Mehmet after the capture of Constantinople.

Question Time

1 How powerful does the Ottoman Empire seem to be by the end of the sixteenth century? Look back at the map on page 161 to see the size of the earlier Islamic Empire and make some comparisons.

2 Which of the four ingredients do you think was most important in
a getting a huge empire?
b keeping it safe?

3 One Ottoman sultan called Selim doubled the size of the empire in just eight years. Another murdered all his brothers (there were 19 of them). What else can you find out about the power of the Ottoman sultans? Here are some key names and other words to help you with your research: Selim I, Mehmet II, harem, Suleyman, vizier, Selim II, The Battle of Lepanto, Mehmet III.

4 Were all the Ottoman sultans wise generals and leaders?

THE POWER OF THE SULTAN

The most famous of all Ottoman sultans was Suleyman the Magnificent. Under his rule the Ottoman Empire was at its largest. The most obvious question to ask is why he had such an impressive title. After Suleyman the power and strength of the Ottoman Empire began to slowly decline. It had almost become too large to control.

Suleyman the Magnificent

Suleyman ruled the Ottoman Empire from 1520 to 1566. He spent much of his life at war and invaded many new areas. He got nearly as far north as Vienna, but his armies were stopped by bad weather. He spent huge amounts of money on building amazing palaces, paintings and other luxuries. Suleyman was also called 'the lawmaker' as his government sent out so many orders. He had the reputation of being a very fair man.

Suleyman, like other early Turkish sultans, had a policy of employing talented and able men for jobs as his officials. This way many people worked hard, knowing that if they were clever they would be rewarded. It meant that the empire was well run.

Suleyman's family life caused him some problems. He was worried about who should succeed him as sultan. He had taken the unusual step of actually having a member of his harem as one of his

SOURCE 2

Suleyman became famous all over the world as a great leader. He lived between 1499 and 1566, which is at the same time as King Henry VIII of England (1491–1547).

wives. She was called Roxelana and she wanted her son to be Suleyman's heir, rather than his oldest son. She persuaded Suleyman that his oldest son was not to be trusted. Suleyman had him killed and she got her way. Her son, Selim II, became sultan after Suleyman. Unfortunately he was not a good leader, preferring drinking and eating. After him the sultans were less powerful and less respected, spending their time enjoying the luxuries of their wealth rather than fighting and protecting their empire.

SOURCE 3

A painting of Henry VIII, painted by Hans Holbein the Younger in the sixteenth century.

Henry VIII – a similar ruler?

Henry VIII ruled for 38 years. He worked hard to make England a more powerful country. He was helped by advisers such as Cardinal Wolsey, Thomas More and Thomas Cromwell. Henry is famous for breaking away from the Pope and setting up his own Church of England. This gave the English kings and queens (monarchs) power over religion a well as politics (ruling) and economics (money). Henry closed down the monasteries which were a threat to his power. This meant that he gained a huge amount of extra wealth, which he spent on feasts, paintings, clothes and entertainment. He is also famous for having six different wives, and executing two of them. Above all, Henry wanted the Tudor family to be strong monarchs. He wanted to have a son to succeed him

and so he divorced his first wife because she was too old to have any more children. His third wife had a son who succeeded him as Edward VI. Edward, however, was not a strong King. He was ill and died at the age of 15.

Henry stayed popular with his most of his people, but wars with France and Scotland towards the end of his reign were expensive and Henry killed anyone who opposed him. This included Catholics and Protestants, and even some of his advisers, including Thomas More and Thomas Cromwell. He did increase the importance of England in Europe, but did not gain much extra land. Henry ended up with the reputation of a tyrant who always got his way.

SOURCE 4

A modern photo of the interior of Suleyman's mosque at Edirne, built in the sixteenth century.

Question Time

❶ How similar is Suleyman's mosque to Source 2 on page 172?

❷ You may already know a lot about Henry VIII. Use all your knowledge to compare him with Suleyman the Magnificent. Here are some key aspects for you to look at when you make your comparison:

    appearance
    intelligence
    lands ruled
    wealth and lifestyle
    respect and fear of his people.

Make a big list of the main similarities and differences between these two rulers.

❸ Write up your findings in paragraphs. You can use these sentence starts if you like.

Henry VIII and Suleyman the Magnificent were both famous rulers. They........

They had some things in common. ......

But they were also very different men......

I think that they have more similarities/differences because.....

I think that Suleyman/Henry was the greater leader because..............

A THOUSAND YEARS OF ISLAMIC CIVILISATION, 600-1600

To show how much you have learned about the Islamic states in this Unit, you are to produce, as part of a team working on an Internet Encyclopaedia for 11-13 years olds, a Web page to describe the main aspects of Islamic civilisation. The page will be used by other students researching this topic. You will have to chose and write your material very carefully, using ICT, if you are able. The best pages will look good, but also contain lots of helpful information.

INSTRUCTIONS

Each Web page must include four different parts:

1   An introduction as to why this period of Islamic history is so important in world history.

2   A paragraph or series of paragraphs about different aspects of Islamic civilisation. Split them up into headings and subheadings if you can.

3   One picture to go with the writing, with several sentences explaining what it shows us about Islamic achievements.

4   One single picture for a title page, which for you best sums up the achievements made by the Islamic states in this period. Under this summary picture you will need to finish this sentence: 'For me this picture really sums up what the Islamic Empire achieved between 600 and 1600 because........'

Step 1 Choose some aspects of Islamic history on which to base your Web page. Your teacher may tell you which aspects to focus on and whether to work alone or in small groups or pairs. There are some suggestions for different headings in the box below.

Architecture	Maths and science	Creating an empire	The caliphs
Famous cities	A civilised way of life	The Crusades	
Famous Muslims	The Ottomans	A world religion and way of life	

Step 2 Look back through your notes on this Unit and other pages in this book, and pick out the main points that you want to include in your writing. Remember to choose your words and pictures carefully. You could copy and paste your pictures from an encyclopaedia. You could always create arrows and label different parts of your picture.